No More Empty H

Dr. Leroy Thompson, Sr.

No More Empty Hands!
First Edition
ISBN 978-1-931804-38-7

Copyright © 2008 by Dr. Leroy Thompson, Sr.
Ever Increasing Word Ministries
P. O. Box 7
Darrow, Louisiana 70725

Published by Ever Increasing Word Ministries.
P. O. Box 7
Darrow, Louisiana 70725

Table of Contents

Introduction

It is my privilege as a minister of the Gospel to teach people that the God I represent has the ability to meet the needs of the multitude, yet He can supply the answer to each individual's need, satisfying his hunger and fulfilling his dreams.

It is unequivocally God's will to prosper you and fill your hands with plenty — to supply you in such a way that you have no lack of any kind. I can say that boldly and with great confidence because I've lived it. I *know* what will happen when you obey God with all of your heart and receive His Word as precious because you know it's the only thing that can truly change your life.

Some try to change their financial condition by going back to school to further their education or by working a second or third job. Neither of these things is wrong in itself. But you can't bypass spiritual laws and still expect a spiritual harvest. If you want God's highest and best for your life, the only way out of your situation is to cooperate with His laws and to do things *His* way. Then with enduring trust, you can expect the Lord to deliver you. And He will!

In this book, I use some terms that I have not used before, but God gave them to me in prayer, and they are powerful. Sometimes just one word, or one statement, can change a person's mind, heart, and life completely! When the anointing is on your words, those words have the power to demolish strongholds and to bring light and blessing in areas where a person was once in darkness and despair.

Always remember that God can fill your hands and change your situation in the blink of an eye. But He starts on the inside, in your heart. In other words, *prosperity* is a *process*. My prayer is that the words in this book will bring you into greater and greater financial freedom as God fills your hands with plenty and teaches you how to *keep* them filled to overflowing with divine prosperity.

CHAPTER ONE

No More Empty Hands — The Will of God For You!

To lay a proper foundation for what I'm going to share in this book, I must first discuss the will of God concerning our prosperity and well-being in life. Even if you've been taught that God is a good God and a loving Father, who desires to meet the needs of His children, I want you to read each word in this chapter as if you've never heard the message before.

Part of my job as a minister is to connect people to the will of God for their lives. When they learn how to make that connection through their faith and obedience, great things will occur, such as when Jesus fed thousands with one boy's lunch, a Bible story you're probably familiar with. Jesus fed all of those people using spiritual laws — not any natural law — and we are going to look at some of those spiritual laws in the pages of this book.

God has a lot to say about money. He talked about it in the Old Testament. Jesus talked about it in His earthly ministry. And holy men of God wrote about it in the Epistles as they were inspired by the Holy Ghost.

Wanting, Wishing, and Waiting

So why haven't we been hearing what the Lord has to say? I mean *really* hearing. Because if we had been *hearing* more, we would have been *having* more. Instead, we have been wanting, wishing, and waiting. The saying bears repeating here: We are not waiting on *God* — He is waiting on *us!*

God wants you blessed! Just as He wants you healed, He wants you financially blessed.

"Then why are so many believers struggling financially?" you might ask.

Just because prosperity is the will of God for all doesn't mean that every person will walk in the light of that truth and enjoy financial success. Similarly, just because healing is the will of God for all doesn't mean everyone is going to walk in the light of *healing* and live in divine health.

Finally, salvation — eternal redemption — is the will of God for all, but that doesn't mean that every person will choose to believe on Jesus Christ as Savior and receive that salvation. Some will abide eternally in hell, yet that is not the will of God for any one of them (2 Peter 3:9)!

I realize that many Christians have been struggling financially. They've been squeezing and scratching to make ends meet! But it is unnecessary. That is not God's plan for their lives. Poverty and financial lack do not come from God, nor are they the will of God. For every scripture some naysayer could quote to try to make poverty sound holy, I can quote many, many more that reveal God's willingness to see us prosper and do well in life.

It is God's nature to bless and to prosper. And not only is He *willing* to prosper us, He is *able* to do it! God is not broke. Jesus isn't broke! And the Holy Ghost isn't broke, either! So what are you waiting for? It's time for you to take a stand and make a bold declaration today, *"No more empty hands!"*

The Blessing of Plenteousness Versus Empty-Handedness

Hold your hands out in front of you and look at them. Those hands were made by God to do a work for Him in the earth realm. Now, I'm going to ask you a question. Can you do much of anything, including work for God, with *empty hands* — with hands that are empty of finances? No, it takes money to operate in the earth. And God wants to fill your hands with the finances you need to accomplish the tasks He assigns and to live well as His representative. He wants to give you handfuls of "plenty."

Your hands need to be full in order to fulfill God's purposes. Maybe you thought it was all about you and your family and your needs, but it's not. What you need, want, and dream about is important, as we will see. But money has a purpose, a *main purpose*. And that purpose is the propagation of the Good News of the Gospel — reaping the harvest of men's souls, making disciples, and teaching all nations (*see* Matthew 28:19). There are things God has prepared for people that they won't receive unless someone pays for it.

Someone said, "Yes, but I thought the Gospel was free."

The Gospel is free, but it costs money to "go"!

As I said, your needs and desires are important to God. Having your needs met and your personal dreams fulfilled are part of the package. But in order to begin walking in this realm of financial blessing, *first*, you're going to have to understand money's first purpose: the propagation of the Gospel and the saving of souls. *Second,* you're going to have to be firmly established in the will of God concerning your financial prosperity. You're going to have to recognize that God doesn't want you going through life as a beggar or even barely getting by. He doesn't want you wearing His Name as His child and living like He doesn't take care of you!

What Is the Lord Saying to His People Concerning Money?

I believe the Lord is calling His people to come up higher than they've ever been before in their revelation of His goodness and His ability to bless us financially. I'm going to show you in this book how you can know the will of God for yourself in such a way that you will receive in your heart and declare for your own life, "No more empty hands for me!"

God has spoken in His Word on this subject, and He is speaking into the lives of many today to stir ourselves up and receive what He is saying to us about money.

> *Exodus 3:21*
> *And I will give this people favour in the sight of the Egyptians: and it shall come to pass, that, when ye go, YE SHALL NOT GO EMPTY:*

In this verse, the Lord is telling Moses about the future exodus of the children of Israel from Egypt. I want you to particularly notice the phrase in verse 21 that indicates *in what condition* they would leave their captivity. God said, *"Ye shall not go empty."*

Let's look at another verse that further proves how the Lord feels about His people being empty-handed.

Exodus 23:15

Thou shalt keep the feast of unleavened bread: (thou shalt eat unleavened bread seven days, as I commanded thee, in the time appointed of the month Abib; for in it thou camest out from Egypt: and NONE SHALL APPEAR BEFORE ME EMPTY.

God doesn't want you to come before Him empty-handed — without seed to sow into His Kingdom and His work. Why? Because those empty hands rob Him of the pleasure of returning financial blessings to you and of keeping those hands full for His purposes and for His glory. Your sowing is God's means of multiplying harvest unto you, as we will look at in greater detail in another chapter.

Let's look at one more verse that reveals God's feelings concerning empty-handedness.

Deuteronomy 15:13

And when thou sendest him out free from thee, THOU SHALT NOT LET HIM GO AWAY EMPTY.

In this verse, God was commanding His people regarding the treatment of their slaves who were fellow Hebrews. He said that after a man's Hebrew brother had served him six years, he was to let him go free and not send him away empty-handed. God wanted something in that man's hands so he could begin a life for himself and his family that would glorify God. As I said, God doesn't want one of His children living like He isn't taking care of him.

This verse in Deuteronomy 15 shows us the association between freedom and having something in your hands. God associates finances with freedom. There has been too much financial captivity in the Body of Christ, and God wants to turn that around. The Lord does not want His people empty-handed!

Exodus 3:21-22, Exodus 23:15, and Deuteronomy 15:13 tell me three things about wealth or finances:

1. God did not intend that you "go out" of spiritual captivity empty-handed.

In other words, when you became born again, God did not intend that you go through the rest of your life broke, full of lack and insufficiency, and with dreams you can't pay for. He wants your hands full — not full of lack but of plenty!

2. God does not want you to come before Him with empty hands.

God, who gives seed to the sower (2 Corinthians 9:10), does not want you without seed to sow. Since this is His will, if you will purpose in your heart to obey Him in faith, He has a responsibility to put something into your hands to sow into His Kingdom.

3. God wants your hands full of wealth so that He can call on you as a co-laborer with Him to help finance His work to reap the precious fruit of the earth (James 5:7) — the harvest of men's and women's souls — and to teach them (Matthew 28:19).

Without seed in your hands, God cannot fulfill His financial purposes in you. But when you have seed, and you sow that seed in cooperation with Him, He can establish His covenant of prosperity with you.

I believe the days are coming to an end when the Church has to go to the world for finances. The world should be coming to the Church! The heathen had better laugh as loud as they can now, because I read in my Bible that *"...the wealth of the sinner is laid up for the just"* (Proverbs 13:22).

The following verses also speak about transferals of wealth.

Job 27:16-17
16 Though he [the wicked man] heap up silver as the dust, and prepare raiment as the clay;
17 He may prepare it, but the just shall put it on, and the innocent shall divide the silver.

Ecclesiastes 2:26
For God giveth to a man that is good in his sight wisdom, and knowledge, and joy: but to the sinner he giveth travail, to gather and to heap up, THAT HE MAY GIVE TO HIM THAT IS GOOD BEFORE GOD....

God is going to see to it that every promise He has spoken will come to pass in the lives of those who are *"good before God...."*

Paid For by Blood

Your hands being filled with God's financial blessing is a divine privilege that was paid for by Blood. The blood of Jesus ratified a covenant of wholeness that you now have with God if you are His child. It doesn't matter what color your skin is, nor your family history or academic background. Not one of those things is an issue — our covenant is the issue!

So the blood of Jesus has something to do with your hands! His blood has something to do with your prosperity!

We have been redeemed from the curse of the Law (Galatians 3:13). That means that through the work of Christ in redemption, the curse of the Law — poverty, sickness, and spiritual death — has been broken over our lives. Redemption is where it all began. Now you have to "finish" it by becoming an actual recipient of that which God has purchased, provided, and intended for you to have.

Second Corinthians 8:9 says, *"For ye know the grace of our Lord Jesus Christ, that, though he was rich, yet for your sakes he became poor, that ye through his poverty might be rich."*

Some people read that verse and get religious about it, saying, "Through His spiritual poverty, you have become rich *with grace*." Then they want you to shout about that as if nothing else matters. But after you're done shouting, and the emotion leaves you, you still need some groceries! You need some *money*!

Certainly, God's saving grace is the most important thing, because without it, we would be condemned to hell — to eternal damnation. But let me tell you, Heaven can be your eternal destination, yet if you go through life "broke," you're simply not going to have a lot of joy, *especially* if you know that prosperity is the will of God for you!

Have you ever heard it said that no one is as miserable on this earth as a backslidden believer? A backslider is miserable because he knows he's not living right. He knows things are supposed to be better, yet he's not taking hold of the things of God or experiencing them personally.

Likewise, a Christian who sees the light concerning divine prosperity and begins to have some understanding that God wants him blessed cannot be completely joyful if he goes month after month and year after year broke, struggling, and barely making it. Once he knows the will of God for his life, nothing will satisfy him except to walk in the light of it and enjoy God's highest and best.

Receive the Message

The stench of religion and doctrines of men and devils have covered this revelation of divine prosperity with a shroud. The spiritual blindness on the hearts and minds of many in the Body of Christ must be dealt with, and the only way to deal with error is with truth.

There is so much fog and smog that has been placed over the truth of this message that we teachers of the Word have to "hammer" the truth over and over again. People don't always hear you the first time — that is, they don't hear you with *spiritual* ears. In other words, people don't always "get" the truth and understand it the first time they hear it.

Actually, only a remnant is ever going to "get it." Only a percentage is going to take hold of the message fully. Many are going to say the message is not from God, ignoring scripture after scripture that declare otherwise. Then they will go on and depend on their education, on working two jobs, or on credit cards and bank loans to make it in life.

Some Christians balk at this message because they say that their needs are met, and they are content; they don't want anything else. But they should hear the message and receive it so God can use their hands for His purposes! They should walk in the light of the Word so that God can use them to bless others.

And believing the message is not hard. People believe that God can take them to Heaven, heal their bodies, and protect their children and families. So why can't they believe Him to fill their hands?

If you would permit the Holy Spirit to impress upon your spirit that this is not just some off-the-wall message, you would rise to a higher level in your understanding, in your faith, and in your ability to receive what God has so freely given. You will realize that it is your right and privilege to live in prosperity and wealth. Once you do see it, if you will stay with it, the message will ring louder and louder in your spirit. You will become so strong in faith that no one will be able to talk you out of it. And you will *have* what belongs to you!

God Is the God of Fulfilled Dreams

God wants His people blessed — not just a few in the Body, but *all of us*. And not just ministers, but laity too. God is no respecter of persons (*see* Acts 10:34). He doesn't just want to bless the preacher; He wants to bless *every* member of the Body of Christ.

Think about it. The Lord knew you before you were born (*see* Jeremiah 1:5). He had certain good works laid out ahead of time for you to do and a certain path for you to walk on (Ephesians 2:10). He has put dreams in your heart. And He is not the God of broken dreams, but of dreams *fulfilled*.

Do you realize that dreams on this earth cost something? Have you ever heard the expression, "This is our dream house." Those people paid something for that dream home. You could also have a dream car, a dream vacation, and so forth, but all of it costs something.

The reason some people have lacked good things in life is they have never dreamed big enough. They have not dared to admit their deepest dreams and desires. Instead, some have lied about it, saying, "I don't want much of anything in life. I'm just going to serve the Lord." Unless a person is crazy or crippled in his mind, *everyone* on this planet wants *something*!

Instead of attending a service hungry to walk in more light from the Word, some people treat every service like it's an "I-just-love-the-Lord meeting"! (But after they get done loving the Lord, they need to go out and do something for Him — and they're going to need some money to do it!)

If these people would just be truthful and willing to go against the grain of tradition just a little bit, God could help them. He could talk to them and begin to teach them some things. Instead, many choose to remain entrenched in religious tradition and the doctrines of men.

If you open your heart to God and ask Him to teach you, He will do it! He will set you up and position you to receive His highest and best, because that is His will for you. It pleases Him when we seek Him eagerly and allow ourselves to be taught by men and women of God who have gone before us and through faith and patience inherited — received and enjoyed — certain promises.

I am enjoying the fulfillment of "prosperity promises" in my life today because I dared to take God at His Word. I obeyed His written Word, and I also obeyed the voice of His Spirit when He would speak to me about something He wanted me to do. I obey Him to this day.

The Will of God and the Pathway of New Beginnings

The Lord is so well-pleased when His children accept the invitation to change their way of thinking and their way of living. This change can only come about as they receive the truth of the Word.

For example, the truth of the Word concerning divine prosperity will cause a believer to become less job-oriented and more principle-oriented because he sees that the principle will outdo the job. He will become less self-oriented and more principle-oriented because he understands that the principle will take him out far beyond himself and enable him to help others.

What about you? What principles do you live by? When the principle is from the Word of God, it will help put you over in every situation of life if you'll apply yourself to it.

God doesn't want any among the Body of Christ today to be empty-handed, just as He didn't want the children of Israel to leave the place of their captivity empty-handed. I believe God is saying to believers today, "No more empty hands!"

Walking In the Financial Favor of God

Have you ever said, "I know I could get ahead financially if I could just get a bigger raise this year," or, "We'll be okay financially if the stock market would just stay steady," or, "I could pay for Christmas this year without going into debt if I could just get enough overtime at my job"?

It's true, you could benefit to some degree if the things of this world were more predictable. But this world's system is anything *but* predictable! And it's only designed to make a few people rich. It leaves most people hanging on the line, *wishing* they could be rich. It leaves them chanting, "If only I could do *this* or *that*, then I would be rich too."

The Bible warns against trusting, or putting your hope, in "uncertain riches" (1 Timothy 6:17). They are as uncertain as the wind — finances could be flowing in one direction one minute, and in another direction the next!

Then what *can* cause you to get ahead financially? I mean, *way* ahead, where you'd never have to be concerned with your retirement years or about paying for Christmas this year. I know something that can do all of these things. It's the financial favor of God.

As I said in the Introduction, I'm going to use some terms in this book that I've never used before, terms that the Lord gave me in prayer. But these terms are thoroughly scriptural — they can absolutely be backed up and supported by the Word of God. And one of those terms is "financial favor."

When I first began using the words "financial favor" in my meetings, I'd never heard them used together like this. But I see financial favor in Scripture.

Many in the Body of Christ have been broke, struggling, and barely making it by financially. But there is a cure for that condition. The cure for empty hands is to be positioned to receive the *financial favor* of God.

God has provided us with financial favor — He has made this "cure" available to each one of us. But we cannot utilize this cure without first gaining some knowledge about God's *will* and His *ways* concerning the financial favor of God.

Psalm 102:13
Thou shalt arise, and have mercy upon Zion: FOR THE TIME TO FAVOUR HER, YEA, THE SET TIME, IS COME.

I'm talking about financial favor within the context of the covenant God has established for us in Christ after the order of Abraham. I don't know how we as the Body of Christ have overlooked it for so long, believing God for everything else but favor — for just our little needs met here and there.

When I received the revelation of "Money Cometh" from the Lord more than ten years ago, I'd never heard that term, either. There were seemingly only a handful of ministers teaching on divine prosperity. In fact, in the denomination I had come out of, you never heard much at all about money from God's perspective. But that never bothered me. I knew I'd received that revelation from the Lord.

Years ago, it seemed as if the only mention of money from the pulpit occurred during the offering. But what little people heard during the offering didn't build their faith, strengthen their beliefs, or help their financial situation in the least.

You can talk about the offering all you want, but if people don't understand financial favor, they won't sow properly, and they won't reap properly, either. They won't experience the financial increase that God wants them to have in life.

To Receive God's Financial Favor, You Must Realize That He Is Your Source

Before you can receive financial favor from God, you're going to have to establish Him as your source. If you're still looking for favor from the world, your faith will be misguided, and you will become disillusioned in your thinking.

We as Christians have become mixed up as to our source in life. Academia is not our source. There's nothing wrong with education, but your education cannot become your source. Your job or your rich relative cannot become your source.

When I talk about financial favor, I'm not talking about just paying a house note. I'm talking about a great deal more than that! God said to those who sowed financial seed in the Philippian church, *"But my God shall supply all your need according to his riches in glory by Christ Jesus"* (Philippians 4:19).

15

First, the Holy Spirit said through Paul that God would meet all their need because they were givers. But then the Lord said something else about *how* He was going to meet that need: *"...according to his riches in glory by Christ Jesus."* When God says He's going to bless you according to His own resources, *that's* financial favor!

Do you understand the vast expansiveness of the statement, *"...according to his riches in glory by Christ Jesus"*? Do you know how much clout that phrase holds? That phrase isn't referring to any check from your job — it's not even referring to a large amount of wealth. It's talking about resources that are completely limitless!

Let's look at another verse that talks about the expansiveness of God.

Ephesians 3:20
Now unto him that is able to do EXCEEDING ABUNDANTLY ABOVE all that we ask or think, according to the power that worketh in us.

The phrase, *"...exceeding abundantly above all that we ask or think...,"* is the measure of your source when you establish God as your source. In order to make that connection, however, and experience the financial favor of God, you're going to have to be convinced of His will for you concerning favor for finances. You have to understand that this kind of wealth is available to you and that God will fill your hands with wealth if you will permit Him to do it.

Your understanding of God's will generates the connection to His wealth. The connection in turn creates the proper current or flow. Then that current supplies the power to change your situation and to bring to pass the impossible in your life. Your financial favor and the turning of your financial captivity will take place "according to the power that is able to work through you" as you believe and trust!

To Receive God's Financial Favor, You Must Realize How Much God Loves You

To receive favor from God, including financial favor, not only do you have to establish God as your source, you have to recognize the great love He has for you.

Some people in the Church have stayed broke simply because they don't recognize how much God loves them. That's one of the reasons the Body of Christ has gone to the world for help getting their needs met.

> *Romans 8:37-39*
> *37 Nay, in all these things we are more than conquerors through him THAT LOVED US.*
> *38 For I am persuaded, that neither death, nor life, nor angels, nor principalities, nor powers, nor things present, nor things to come,*
> *39 Nor height, nor depth, nor any other creature, shall be able to separate us FROM THE LOVE OF GOD, which is in Christ Jesus our Lord.*

You need to go off by yourself in a corner of your house and dance just because God loves you! Then say out loud, "I don't care what the condition looks like. God loves me! He is my source and He loves me!"

Because you are in Christ, God favors you this day. Meditate on that truth and let it sink deep into your understanding. Then begin to expect the favor of God to work wonders in your life.

To Receive God's Favor, You Must Understand His 'Blessing System'

We've already looked at two areas in which we must gain understanding if we want to walk in financial favor: (1) We must establish God as our source; and (2) we must understand how much God loves us.

Number *three*, if we want to receive the financial favor of God, we must understand His plan of systematically blessing us, or His "blessing system."

Part One of the Blessing System: *Separate*

To walk in God's favor, there may be times He will ask you to separate yourself from some people, some habits, some beliefs, and so forth in order to walk just with Him and with those who will approach His Word with an open and sincere heart to receive truth.

Some Christians will hear a verse, such as Philippians 4:19, and shout, "Amen! That's true! Preach it!" But that verse is not real to them. They're only hearing it with their *physical* ears. They're not hearing with their *spiritual* ears, listening to the Holy Spirit speak to their spirit about that verse of Scripture.

Some Christians can't hear God's voice because the voice of their pastor rings so loudly in their hearing. For years, these dear believers have been indoctrinated by their pastors' beliefs that don't line up with the Word of God. Now their eyes and ears are dimmed and dampened where the truth is concerned.

Others are too influenced by relatives who are set in their ways of thinking. They cut themselves off from the financial favor of God, because Grandma So-and-So says it ain't so!

Do you know someone like that? You can't talk him out of his unbelief, yet he continually does his level best to talk you out of your faith.

God may require you to separate yourself from these people. If not physically, He may require you to turn your back on their unbelieving ways so that you may follow Him more fully.

Let's look at a man who made a clean break from his past when the Lord spoke to him about a future filled with favor.

Genesis 12:1-4
1 Now the Lord had said unto Abram, Get thee out of thy country, and from thy kindred, and from thy father's house, unto a land that I will shew thee:
2 And I will make of thee a great nation, and I will bless thee, and make thy name great; and thou shalt be a blessing:
3 And I will bless them that bless thee, and curse him that curseth thee: and in thee shall all families of the earth be blessed.
4 So Abram departed, as the Lord had spoken unto him....

Let's look at Genesis 12:1 in *The Amplified Bible.*

Genesis 12:1 (Amplified)
Now [in Haran] *the Lord said to Abram, Go for yourself* [for your own advantage] *away from your country, from your relatives and your father's house, to the land that I will show you.*

Notice this version reads, "Go for yourself, for your own advantage...." Sometimes God can't show favor to people as He desires until they go *for* themselves *from* something that would hold them back from the fullness of His blessings.

Personally, in order to enter God's systematic plan for blessing me, I had to turn away from both some kinfolk and some religious folk. That was years ago. God was beginning to teach me certain truths from His Word, but every time I shared with some of these people what God was saying to me, they tried to talk me out of it.

Look at the wisdom of the Holy Spirit through David in Psalm 1.

Psalm 1:1-3
1 Blessed is the man that walketh not in the counsel of the ungodly, nor standeth in the way of sinners, nor sitteth in the seat of the scornful.
2 But his delight is in the law of the Lord; and in his law doth he meditate day and night.
3 And he shall be like a tree planted by the rivers of water, that bringeth forth his fruit in his season; his leaf also shall not wither; and whatsoever he doeth shall prosper.

The last words of this passage read, *"...and whatsoever he doeth shall prosper."* Why don't we see more of this happening? Because if we want to walk in this kind of favor and blessing from the Lord, we're going to have to do what verse 1 says. We can't receive ungodly counsel and at the same time try to walk in the godly counsel of God's Word. If we keep company with those who oppose God's Word or who won't take a stand on it, their unbelief *will* have an affect on us (Proverbs 13:20).

Also, if we are keeping company with scorners or mockers, we will suffer the consequences when we look for the favor of God. We are prevented from taking hold of it because of wrong words we allowed to enter our ears and get into our heart and mind.

Make no mistake about it. The wrong kind of company will corrupt you (1 Corinthians 15:33)! It will keep you out of the realm of God's favor and remove you from God's systemic plan of blessing you.

Part Two of the Blessing System: *Show*

God's systematic plan of blessing is designed to bring you from one level to the next. God doesn't want you to stay in one place in your finances or in *any* area of your life. He is always calling you up higher — to a better marriage, a stronger family, a more effective ministry or vocation, and to hands that overflow with plenty, because of His financial favor!

But just because God is calling every believer doesn't mean that each one will answer. There is a price to pay to get in on the "system" and to walk in God's best. First, you must *separate* from those people and things that would try to turn you away from obeying God — whether from friends, relatives, and religious leaders, or even from excessive time spent on television, hobbies, or forms of entertainment that would distract you from the things of God.

Then after you've separated yourself, or set yourself apart, and you're walking in the blessings of God, the next level in God's blessing plan is to *show* you off to others — to display His glory in you so that others can look at you and say, "I want what you have! And you can show them the way.

Didn't God put His man Abraham on display for the world to see? To this day, Abraham is known as the father of our faith and as a faithful follower and friend of God, a man that entered solemnly into a covenant with God Almighty, kept his part of the covenant, and was overwhelmed with God's best as God mightily kept *His* part!

Now let's look at Genesis 12:2 in *The Amplified Bible*.

Genesis 12:2 (Amplified)
And I will make of you a great nation, and I will bless you [with abundant increase of favors] and make your name famous and distinguished, and you will be a blessing [dispensing good to others].

After I began to prosper, some of the same people who belittled my faith and tried to talk me out of divine prosperity years ago said to me, "Leroy, you knew all along where you were headed, didn't you."

I thought of the way Abram left his hometown in obedience to God and didn't even know where he was going, and I answered those people, "I was just being led by the Spirit of God."

If you're serious about getting in on God's "blessing system," God will *separate* you and then *show* you off to others that He might be glorified (*see* Isaiah 61:3). And you will have handfuls of *plenty* to show for it!

How One Woman Qualified For Financial Favor and Received 'Handfuls of Purpose'

Now I want to look at the life of a girl who got in on God's blessing system and walked in tremendous financial favor.

I'm talking about Ruth, a Moabite woman, who married Mahlon, a Jew and the son of Elimelech and Naomi. Elimelech died, and his son, Ruth's husband, also died. Elimelech's other son, Chilion, who was married to a girl by the name of Orpah, died too.

You can read this interesting account in the Book of Ruth, but in summary, I will tell you that after all of that dying going on and after suffering so much loss, Naomi decided to return to Judah, the land of her own people. Orpah stayed with her relatives in Moab, but Ruth chose to follow her mother-in-law, saying, "... *whither thou goest, I will go; and where thou lodgest, I will lodge: thy people shall be my people, and thy God my God: Where thou diest, will I die, and there will I be buried: the Lord do so to me, and more also, if ought but death part thee and me*" (Ruth 1:16-17).

Determined, Devoted, and Rewarded

Ruth and Naomi arrived in Bethlehem, destitute. Ruth got a job working in the fields of a man named Boaz, where her job was to glean leftovers — sheaves left behind by the reapers.

> *Ruth 2:15-16*
> *15 And when she [Ruth] was risen up to glean, Boaz commanded his young men, saying, Let her glean even among the sheaves, and reproach her not:*
> *16 And let fall also some of the HANDFULS OF PURPOSE for her, and leave them, that she may glean them, and rebuke her not.*

Ruth *separated* herself from her family and friends and left her hometown to follow her mother-in-law to a foreign country! But Ruth recognized that Naomi served the One true God, and Ruth vowed to follow both Naomi and her God.

I'm sure it was hard on Ruth traveling from Moab to Judah while taking care of her mother-in-law. Then Ruth took a job working hard in the fields so that she and her mother-in-law could eat. But Ruth was determined and devoted, and from there, she was rewarded — she went from receiving "handfuls of purpose" from a godly man of wealth to becoming a matriarch in the bloodline of Jesus!

God will give you favor, too, when you're devoted to Him and to the truth of His Word. When you're willing to pay the price to obey and follow Him, as did Abraham and Ruth, God will rain financial favor on your life and fill your hands with plenty!

Favor Will Fill Your Hands and Spoil Your Enemies

When God first told Moses that he would lead the Israelites out of Egypt, He said to Moses, "You shall not go empty."

What set the children of Israel up for this to come to pass? What set them up to be delivered from their captivity with hands that were full? *The favor of God.*

Exodus 3:21
And I will give this people FAVOUR in the sight of the Egyptians: and it shall come to pass, that, when ye go, ye shall not go empty.

God told Moses, "I will give this people favor." Notice He didn't say, "I will give them two jobs."

Well, how did He favor them then? Verse 22 tells us.

Exodus 3:22
But every woman shall borrow of her neighbour, and of her that sojourneth in her house, jewels of silver, and jewels of gold, and raiment: and ye shall put them upon your sons, and upon your daughters; and ye shall spoil the Egyptians.

God gave financial favor to His people by having them request items of silver, gold, and raiment of their Egyptian masters. As they obeyed the word of the Lord, they didn't get trinkets in return for their asking. No, the things they received caused them to "spoil" the Egyptians. In other words, the

Egyptians lost their wealth that day. It was a divine transaction wrought by the favor of God that rested on His people.

There are going to be some divine transactions take place in the Body of Christ too — that means they will happen in *your* life! Because of God's favor on your life, people will give you favor that you never had before. Someone might show you favor with a check for $5,000 or with a check to pay off your house or car.

In the following verses, we can see the Israelites obeying and carrying out the word of the Lord through Moses.

> *Exodus 12:35-36*
> *35 And the children of Israel did ACCORDING TO THE WORD OF MOSES; and they borrowed of the Egyptians jewels of silver, and jewels of gold, and raiment:*
> *36 And the Lord gave the people FAVOUR in the sight of the Egyptians, so that they lent unto them such things as they required. And they spoiled the Egyptians.*

First, notice that the children of Israel acted *according to the word of Moses.* In other words, Moses had received a word from the Lord in Exodus 3:21-22 and delivered it to the people of God. The people received it, obeyed it (Exodus 12:35), and were blessed accordingly — according to their faith and obedience: *"And the Lord gave the people favour in the sight of the Egyptians, so that they lent unto them such things as they required. And they* [God's people] *spoiled the Egyptians"* (verse 36).

Notice who received favor as a result of their obedience: *the people.* Moses received the word, or command, of the Lord and delivered that word to the people. But it was the people who benefited as they obeyed God's words as spoken through the man of God.

25

The same is true today. As God's people today have respect for the Word of God as ministered from the mouths of His ministers, they will benefit from the Word that's ministered. As I said, when a true man or woman of God says something to the people of God, he or she is saying it for a reason. When you respond with respect (*see* Second Chronicles 20:20), it gives the Lord the divine privilege of doing something for you that He couldn't do before.

The Power of Financial Favor

The way God completed this transferal of wealth when He delivered the Israelites was not "normal" or natural. Think about it. A slave woman asks her mistress to borrow her jewelry (Exodus 12:35). Under normal circumstances, wouldn't a master say, "You're out of your mind. Get your tail out of my presence!"

But those Egyptian slave-owners couldn't say that, because the Lord was in charge. *He* had sent those slaves — His own people — to their masters to make that strange request. And His people could not be denied, because God's divine favor was upon them to cause them to receive great spoil on their way out of slavery.

I have witnessed with my own eyes people sowing a great seed in obedience to the Holy Spirit's unction and then receiving a promotion worth thousands of dollars. I know of one man who sowed faithfully and received an unheard of raise from his employers. On top of that, they told him to set his own hours, saying, "We just want you with the company."

I get letters and e-mails all the time from people testifying about the great things God is doing in their lives since they got hold of these principles of financial favor.

Are you ready to cooperate with God's laws of favor and receive a financial breakthrough beyond what you've experienced in the past? It doesn't matter how bad things look in your finances, God is your source, and He loves you.

Is your situation a hard case? If so, you are just the person God is looking for! There are no financial impossibilities with God. Second Chronicles 16:9 says, *"For the eyes of the Lord run to and fro throughout the whole earth, to shew himself strong in the behalf of them whose heart is perfect toward him...."* God wants to show Himself strong on behalf of those who walk with Him, fully committed to His Word and His ways.

Friend, it is God's purpose and pleasure to show you financial favor and to prosper you. Won't you receive it and walk in the light of it today?

A Confession For Financial Favor:

"My Father has placed the anointing of favor on my life. Therefore, I fully expect to receive favor from others as I obey Him. I will not reject favor because of false humility. To the contrary, I know that through God's financial favor, I am amply supplied with all that I need and more."

CHAPTER THREE

How To Hold On to Your Dream — The Difference Between Struggling and Suffering

Do you know someone who's struggling financially? I daresay that most of us do. For example, let's say the pastor of your church asked people in the congregation to testify honestly of the financial struggles they were experiencing. You would likely be there all day and night listening to people's stories of how they were struggling in the financial arena.

Most of us are all too familiar with struggling, and we're not familiar enough with escaping and walking free from struggles, burdens, and cares.

We're so familiar with struggling that people even sing songs about the struggles of life. For example, many of the old spirituals were written about struggling. Those songs didn't offer much hope for this life — instead, they focused on the afterlife, on Heaven or the "Sweet By-and-By," when everything would finally be all right. Many black people who were in slavery years ago sang spirituals. But then after they got finished singing, they had to go back into the field!

I don't want to go back into the field! I have escaped the field, and then I escaped the poverty that tried to run after me and hunt me down. And I'm not going back!

Some people love to say trite, trivial things to those who are struggling, such as, "Hold on, the Lord is going to make a way someday."

The Lord has already made a way! Those people who are struggling simply don't have anyone to *show* them the way! Jesus said, "I am the Way, the Truth, the Life" (John 14:6). God made a Way — His Name is Jesus!

Your Response to Struggles

Let's look at that word "struggle" for a moment. When you hear that word, you picture someone bound by something he's trying to escape. So struggles are really nothing to testify about — struggles are for *escaping*!

You never hear people say, "I'm struggling financially, and I'm enjoying it"! No, if they're struggling financially, they're usually doing something to try to escape the position they're in. The only thing they *want* about their struggle is to escape from it!

Are You Struggling or Suffering?

Now I want to show you the difference between struggling and suffering. There's a great difference! Sometimes you'll see someone's circumstances and you'll automatically conclude, "That person is struggling." But he may be *suffering* instead of *struggling*.

Let me explain what I mean. When someone is suffering, yet he's in faith, his suffering is something he endures for a protracted period of time and then it comes to an end. That person who's suffering is actually *enduring* suffering with faith and patience because he has a revelation of God that won't allow him to stay in that condition.

This kind of suffering consists of a period of divine endurance in which you learn divine principles that will help you get out and stay out of that place of suffering. And every step of progress you make is a step out — it's a step in the right direction, a step toward financial favor and freedom.

Characteristics of a Person Who's Enduring by Faith

A person who's suffering today doesn't see himself suffering tomorrow. He's expecting something different. If his condition hasn't changed by morning or by next month, next week, or next year, he's not moved. His attitude and constant confession is, "I may be going through lack now, but I'm going through it with joy because I know I'm coming out of this. In the meantime, I'm obeying the Word of God. I'm not struggling, trying to escape this some other way."

Many in the Body of Christ have been through cycle after cycle of struggling by working several jobs, "borrowing from Peter to pay Paul," looking with desperation for an income-tax refund, and so forth. They make a little progress, but then they fall back. They don't see any way off the treadmill of the world's system that they're on. They're stuck because they don't see the way of escape. They try one thing after another, and they might find a little relief here and there. But eventually, everyone in the family is working to try to make ends meet.

People like this need teaching. They need a revelation from God's Word. They need hope for their future — *Bible* hope — the kind of hope that expects a favorable outcome to their situation.

But many ministers in the Body of Christ have been afraid of this message, and their people are being destroyed as a result because of a lack of knowledge (Hosea 4:6). Other ministers are ignorant of the prosperity message, and their ignorance has trickled down to the members of their congregations.

Enduring the Process

Walking in divine prosperity and living in financial freedom is precious and dangerous at the same time. That's why you must endure *God's way* the financial pressure you may be experiencing instead of looking for a quick fix. You need to learn certain lessons at certain intervals. If you don't, you will never learn what God wants to teach you about handling great sums of money.

For example, without enduring the process, you might come out of your situation spending every dime of your wealth on yourself, forgetting God's main purpose for money. Or you may come out haughty and too proud to ever be taught anything again — not even by God Himself! But if God is not in charge of your life, you'll likely end up in a worse condition, because you didn't endure properly.

When you do something as simple as give when God prompts you to give, and you praise Him even when things look bad, you are growing and learning. Your spirit becomes strengthened by the Word you're hiding in your heart and by your obedience to that Word. The things of this world begin to bother you less and less until the fluctuating economy is no longer a concern. You don't care about the price of gas, groceries, or anything else, because you realize that God is your limitless source.

So what should you do if you find yourself struggling? What should you do if you realize that you're not patiently enduring by faith as you ought to be doing? You ask God for wisdom, and the Lord will give it to you without finding fault with you, without reproaching you, and without saying an unkind word (James 1:5)! Through wisdom, God will show you the way out, so you can escape struggling and learn how to practice enduring.

Why am I making such a big deal about the difference between struggling and suffering? Because if you're *struggling* instead of *suffering*, you're not walking by faith, and you're probably going to keep on struggling. Month after month, year after year, you'll have the same story of struggling to tell. But if you're *enduring*, you're resting and trusting. And although things might look bad now, you know that through your faith and patience, you will inherit or receive and enjoy the fulfillment of the promise.

Hebrews 6:12
That ye be not slothful, but followers of them who through faith and patience inherit the promises.

That's the way the promise of your financial freedom will come — through faith and patience — through learning the lessons of faith and obedience along the way as you endure.

A People In Captivity and In Need of Deliverance

Whenever I mention the words "financial captivity," some people think I'm talking about someone else, not about them.

But if you have bills to pay, and you're cramming money into your bank account as fast as you can get it so you can pay those bills — or so you can cover the checks you've already written — you're in captivity. Or if every time you need something, such as a dress or suit, and you have to use a credit card to pay for it, you're in financial captivity. Even if you have to plan your life around your next paycheck — when you shop for groceries, run errands, get a haircut, eat at a restaurant, or even have company over for dinner — you're in financial captivity.

Most of the Body of Christ is in some sort of financial captivity. The reason I know that is, they can't step out and do what they want to do for the Lord because a lack of finances hinders them. They might try to move out, but they are restrained on all sides. They have to keep their elbows close to their sides, so to speak. They can't swing their arms loose and dance free.

Someone said, "I can dance before the Lord. I don't need money to dance."

Well, can you dance *and* pay? You see, it's one thing to dance and shout because you have a revelation, and you're just waiting for your manifestation. But if you're just dancing to be dancing, you're not completely free, because you don't have a revelation. You don't know in your heart what God wants to do for you concerning money. You're still in financial captivity.

Remember, *your financial captivity is not something you can escape!* It's something you have to endure with patience — by faith in God and His Word — until you come out of it.

Never the Same Again

Enduring your financial captivity is the learning process during which you fully come to understand God's will. The main thing you must learn is that it's not God who's holding you back. Rather, God is setting you up through it all, positioning you so that when come out of your captivity, "you will not go empty," and you will know how never to go back into captivity again!

I wrote a book entitled, *I'll Never Be Broke Another Day in My Life!* [1]. In it, I teach that walking in divine prosperity is not receiving a quick fix here and there when you encounter a financial test or trial. Walking in divine prosperity is a way of life. When you learn certain principles and apply them consistently by faith, you become so bold in your convictions — so dogged and determined about the truth of God's Word in the area of finances — that you *know that you know* you're never going to back to your old way of life again.

All of my money could disappear in a moment, but I'd walk right back into my wealthy place, my place of abundant wealth. Why? Because I've endured some things in life. I've endured having more bills than money to pay them each month. I've endured creditors calling me looking for money. I endured them by faith and didn't try to find my own way of escape. I didn't employ my own methods to get to where I am today. I did things God's way, and I learned my lessons at various intervals — invaluable lessons that have kept me "propped up" and in good standing so that I never have to endure those things again!

Today I live in financial freedom and outright abundance. I live free from concern about whether something is going to get paid on time. I am free to concentrate on other things — and on others. I understand personally, by experience, the phrase "financial favor." Now "financial captivity" is a term of the past for me.

You Were Built To Dream

Many people still don't believe God desires to bless them financially. But God's will is clear. Having your needs abundantly supplied, enjoying the fruit of your labor, receiving your heart's desires — all of those are legitimate blessings that God intends that you have and enjoy. He blesses you with these things through the working of certain spiritual laws, and that's what we're studying in this book: how to work and cooperate with God's laws and principles of increase and freedom.

There's nothing wrong with having your needs met so abundantly that you have a supply, or surplus, left to bless someone else. There's nothing wrong with moving into your dream home without a mortgage attached to it. But people will try to take that away from you. They'll lie, based on things they've heard all their lives about God, saying it's wrong to have these things and that it's wrong to want them.

Do you want something better for yourself than you have today? There's nothing wrong with that! In fact, you were built to have dreams! That's the way God made you. Don't ever let anyone take your dreams away from you.

Hold On to Your Dream

Do you ever daydream of a time in your future that's completely free of financial anxiety and concern? Don't discount that as just a daydream or fantasy. God can position you to march right out of your present condition into a future that's as bright with promise as the noonday sun!

Let's look at a group of people — the children of Israel — that were delivered supernaturally from a terrible bondage.

Psalm 126:1-3
1 When the Lord turned again the captivity of Zion, we were like them that dream.
2 Then was our mouth filled with laughter, and our tongue with singing: then said they among the heathen, The Lord hath done great things for them.
3 The Lord hath done great things for us; whereof we are glad.

This passage is talking about God's people being released from captivity. What does that mean to us today?

Captivity in this country today can be captivity to some sickness or disease or to some other yoke of bondage, such as oppression or depression. People can be financially captive, too, as we have seen. If you still don't believe it, just look at the statistics today concerning the indebtedness of families in this country. People can't have that much debt and be truly free!

Verse 1 says, *"When the Lord turned again the captivity of Zion, we were like them that dream."*

I want you to imagine yourself being delivered from financial captivity or any financial hardship you may be facing today. I'm not talking about some little breakthrough occurring, such as a modest raise at your job or getting a credit-card bill paid off. I'm talking about the kind of breakthrough that causes you to be "as one that dreams."

In other words, imagine that you became so well off financially that you never even had to think about money. Money was just there, waiting on your assignment. That would be like a dream in that it would seem unreal. Yet with God, it can be real.

When God turns our financial captivity, life becomes like a dream in every respect. I had a dream of having no lack or limitation financially, and I am living that dream today.

Do you have a dream? If so, are you trying to make it come true on your own, in your own strength? Or are you permitting God through the principles of His Word to deliver you and turn your captivity? If you will endure the suffering you're experiencing in your situation now by faith and obedience, you will come completely out of that condition and become as one who dreams, because your new life will seem unreal compared to your old way of living.

Forgetting Your Troubles

You can become so permeated with the life and nature of God through your cooperation with His life-giving Word that financial troubles, impossibilities, hopelessness, and despair will become unreal to you! You'll hear others talking about a moody economy and about how they can't do this and they can't do that — and you will hardly know what they're talking about! Life will be as it is described in Job 11:16 (*NIV*), "You will surely forget your trouble, recalling it only as waters gone by."

This won't happen because you escaped your struggling by the skin of your teeth! It will be because you endured some situations by faith and you learned some things. You allowed God's Word to become a part of you, and it changed you. It changed your thinking, your giving, and your priorities concerning money.

Some people will have to endure longer than others before they come out of their suffering, because revelation is progressive. It takes different people different lengths of time to work through some things. How quickly you come out of your suffering actually depends on how much you're willing to pay.

I paid an awesome price to get the breakthroughs financially that I have experienced. And I'm not just talking about sowing financial seed. I paid the price with my heart, my mind, and my body. I gave myself to the meditation of God's Word. I gave myself to total obedience to that Word. I gave myself to intense periods of studying the Word.

All of these things are important when you're enduring a situation by faith, looking for and expecting God to get you out of it and bring you to the place He wants you to be.

Your Deliverance — His Glory

Let's look at Psalm 126:1 again: "*When the Lord turned again the captivity of Zion, we were like them that dream.*" God is able *and willing* to turn things around for you and bring you into your financial dream. So don't ever again doubt that or be afraid to say it. It's not blasphemy to say it — it's *Bible*! It's the right thing to believe and speak, and enduring your suffering by faith in order to live your dream brings glory to Him.

Now let's look at verse 2 of this passage: *"Then was our mouth filled with laughter, and our tongue with singing: then said they among the heathen, The Lord hath done great things for them."*

When your life is like a dream, of course your mouth is going to be filled with laughter and singing. The next part of that verse says, *"…then said they among the heathen…."* The Lord wants to say something among the heathen today. He wants to display His glory and splendor among His people as a calling card to the heathen.

The heathen need to be saved. There's a whole segment of the population on this planet that is on its way to hell. These people are just waiting to hear the Good News so they can believe it and be saved. They need to see the goodness of God in operation and in manifestation in the lives of Christians. And Christians need to be able to fund the ministering of the Gospel on a large scale. It's going to take money to wrap up our commission here on the earth before Jesus comes back.

One of the saddest things in life is not to have enough money to do what you need to do. Having a vision to do something great and not being able to pay for it is not a dream. People say all the time, "Where God guides, He provides." Yes, but is God guiding them? If He is, then He is guiding them in the pages of His Word to walk with Him by faith in His Word and by obedience to what is written.

As God guides you and provides for you, do you know how to handle money, or are you going to start something for Him that you can't finish? You'll be a strong finisher and a victor in every circumstance of life that arises if you'll learn the secret of abiding in Him and enduring in the hard places in life.

The Key To Turning Your Captivity

Let's look at the rest of this passage in Psalm 126.

Psalm 126:4-6
4 Turn again our captivity, O Lord, as the streams in the south.
5 They that sow in tears shall reap in joy.
6 He that goeth forth and weepeth, bearing precious seed, shall doubtless come again with rejoicing, bringing his sheaves with him.

I want you to pay special attention to verse 5, which says, *"They that sow in tears shall reap in joy."*

What are you sowing? If you want to reap a harvest of financial freedom, you're going to have to sow a financial seed. You're also going to have to sow the seed of the Word concerning your financial harvest or blessing.

What Tears and Joy Have In Common

Those who sow in tears shall reap with joy. What do your tears and your joy have in common? The same thing your sowing and reaping have in common: *seed.* You sow seed when you're in financial captivity — and you're still sowing seed when God brings you out and you reap your harvest!

The purpose for your prosperity is the fulfillment of *His* purposes in the earth. At every stage or interval, God is still the giver of seed to the sower, and He is the multiplier of that seed in order to provide bread for the one who has sown — and more seed besides.

I remember when I made up my mind to become a sower of financial seed into God's Kingdom. I told God, "Lord, I'm going to be a sower. I'm going to trust You and take you at Your Word. I know I can't lose with You."

Does that mean it was always easy for me to sow when He told me to sow? No. There times I knew I had to turn some money loose that I really didn't want to turn loose! That's when I had to sow, trusting in the Lord and not leaning not to my own understanding (*see* Proverbs 3:5-6).

When I read Psalm 126:5 and 6, I identify with the phrase "sow in tears," because I've sown finances with a tear in my eye at times! When I sowed my first $100, I said, "Jesus, a whole one-hundred dollars? Are You sure?" But from there, God blessed and increased me. I went on to sow $500 at a time. I sowed in tears, but I reaped in joy!

Doubtless, You Shall Reap

Now look at the last verse in Psalm 126.

Psalm 126:6
He that goeth forth and weepeth, bearing precious seed, shall DOUBTLESS come again with rejoicing, bringing his sheaves with him.

That word "doubtless" in this verse means that *without a doubt*, he who sows his precious seed shall come again with rejoicing, bringing his sheaves — his harvest — with him.

There comes a point when your sowing becomes joyous. I now experience the joy of sowing *and* the joy of reaping. The two joys met because I dared to start with simple acts of obedience, even when it was hard to do those many years ago. I now sow thousands of dollars into God's Kingdom.

I never said enduring would be simple, but it is possible to do it and to do it with joy. With every act of obedience along the way, your trust will deepen more and more. You can endure suffering with patience, and see with your own eyes your captivity turned, your release secured, and your dreams fulfilled — all to the glory of God.

CHAPTER FOUR

Grace For Giving: The Anointing To Sow

I n Chapter 2, I introduced the term "financial favor." In this chapter, I want to share with you another new term: "the sowing anointing," or "the anointing to sow."

The anointing to sow has not been understood in the Body of Christ because it has not been taught properly. Believers, including ministers, have not thought about money in that regard. They have not associated wealth with an anointing. Some think that it's blasphemy to associate wealth — material blessing and prosperity — with the glory of God.

But they can't back that up with Scripture. When you look in the Old Testament at the glory of God that was rained down upon His people to signify His blessing upon their lives, we can read about instances in which prosperity accompanied or followed manifestations of glory. So it's not a sin to think of prosperity as being a blessing from God. In fact, it's a sin to think that prosperity is *not* a blessing of the Lord.

The *anointing* of God is connected with sowing and reaping because the *Word* of God is connected with those principles. Any promise you read in the Word can have the anointing on it if that promise is acted upon and obeyed in faith.

So when I use the phrase "the anointing to sow," I am not sinning! If you were experiencing a financial crisis in your life, and God delivered you from that crisis, He would do it by His Spirit, or by the anointing. The same is true concerning healing for your physical body. If you were sick with a terminal disease, and God healed you and raised you up, He would do it by His Spirit because His Word concerning healing was believed and obeyed, or acted on.

Money Is Spiritual!

The anointing to sow is a vital truth that has been obscured in the Church because we have not really seen this as a spiritual matter. We have equated *money* with the *mundane*.

So much that's wrong has been said and done concerning sowing and reaping until the truth has been almost completely swept away, and truths about God's desire to bless us financially have become like curse words instead of covenant words. But money is a spiritual matter to God!

Giving Grace: The Anointing To Sow

In dealing with this subject of prosperity, I have encountered people who wanted to hear about the anointing to *receive*, but they weren't nearly as excited about the anointing to *give*! They didn't realize that you can't *grow* if you won't *sow*!

Once you have the anointing to sow, the anointing or power to reap becomes very easy. Hands that are anointed to sow are hands that will open up wide to give. No amount God tells you to give will shake you up when your hands become anointed — when you've yielded yourself fully to obey every unction and word from God to sow a seed.

But if your hands can't open up wide to *give*, how are they going to *receive*? The Apostle Paul realized this great truth when he wrote in Second Corinthians 9:6, *"But this I say, He which soweth sparingly shall reap also sparingly; and he which soweth bountifully shall reap also bountifully."*

If you want hands that are full and not empty, you're going to have to do something with the seed you have in your hands.

Seeds That Shout!

We have seen that God does not want you empty-handed. God says what He means and means what He says. And God is not going to embarrass Himself. He can't fail His Word, because He can't fail *Himself*. He and His Word are *one*.

Isaiah 55:11
So shall my [God's] *word be that goeth forth out of my mouth: it shall not return unto me void, but it shall accomplish that which I please, and it shall prosper in the thing whereto I sent it.*

This is what God is saying about His Word: "It shall not return to Me *empty*." The seed of the Word that you sow into your heart, and the seed of finances that you sow according to His Word shall not return empty. When you sow them, both of those seeds are shouting, *"No more empty hands!"*

Sowing Beyond Your Power

Paul wrote a great deal about finances in his writings. Let's look at the following passage in Second Corinthians 8.

45

2 Corinthians 8:1-9

1 Moreover, brethren, we do you to wit of the grace of God bestowed on the churches of Macedonia;

2 How that in a great trial of affliction the abundance of their joy and their deep poverty abounded unto the riches of their liberality.

3 For TO THEIR POWER, I bear record, yea, and BEYOND THEIR POWER they were willing of themselves;

4 Praying us with much intreaty that we would receive the gift, and take upon us the fellowship of the ministering to the saints.

5 And this they did, not as we hoped, but first gave their own selves to the Lord, and unto us by the will of God.

6 Insomuch that we desired Titus, that as he had begun, so he would also finish in you the same grace also.

7 Therefore, as ye abound in every thing, in faith, and utterance, and knowledge, and in all diligence, and in your love to us, see that ye abound in this grace also.

8 I speak not by commandment, but by occasion of the forwardness of others, and to prove the sincerity of your love.

9 For ye know the grace of our Lord Jesus Christ, that, though he was rich, yet for your sakes he became poor, that ye through his poverty might be rich.

In verse 1, Paul is talking about the grace of God to give — a giving grace. In verse 2, Paul says, "From the Macedonians' deep poverty abounded the riches of their liberality." Now, that doesn't even sound right, does it? People who are in deep poverty aren't naturally very liberal or generous.

Verses 3 and 4 say, *"For TO THEIR POWER, I bear record, yea, and BEYOND THEIR POWER they were willing of themselves; Praying us with much intreaty that we would receive the gift, and take upon us the fellowship of the ministering to the saints."*

You might ask, "What does that mean, 'they sowed beyond their power'?" It means the anointing to sow was upon them. They had grace for giving because they were yielded to God, and they were trusting and rejoicing in Him so much that they knew He was going to take care of them and do it in a big way.

The hands of the Macedonians were anointed to sow, and there was power in that. Because of that sowing anointing, that grace for giving, these people who gave to Paul were able to step out beyond their lack and limitations and give as if they weren't broke! They stepped out beyond a poverty mindset and gave liberally toward the preaching of the Gospel.

Now, a person in the same position as the Macedonians wouldn't normally do that. Without the grace for giving, or the anointing to sow, that person's mind would be talking to him and giving him "fits" if he even *thought* about giving something away.

That's why we need to "receive the engrafted Word with meekness" and keep on receiving it until it renews our mind and transforms our life (James 1:21; Romans 12:2). Then when thoughts come, such as, *You still have to pay this, that, and the other,* you'll be trusting God so much, that grace will be greater than any thought, feeling, or suggestion that God is not big enough to multiply finances back to you.

Sowing 'Out of Your Mind'

I call this kind of sowing "sowing like you're out of your mind," because your mind will tell you, *You're nuts! You are out of your mind!* The truth of the matter is, when you're obeying the unction in your spirit to sow, you really *are* sowing "out of your mind" — outside the realm of your mind. You're sowing in the realm of your spirit man, not the realm of your mind.

For example, suppose you have $700 in bills that need to be paid, but you only have $500. Then the Lord tells you to sow $450 into someone's ministry. You *have* to be out of your mind, and in the Spirit, to be able to do that! You have to have some revelation knowledge working in you — some faith and trust to add to your obedience.

That's where the problem has been. Many Christians resist this kind of teaching, and resist the dealings of the Lord to sow and give. They don't want to leave their natural mindset; they want to hold on to figuring, calculating, and trying to pay their bills and get their needs met as best they can.

People like that need an anointing! They need a revelation working in their heart. They need to trust the Holy Spirit and have faith in God that He can bring them out of the financial situation they're in. If they don't make these adjustments, life is going to remain the same for them.

The same Holy Spirit who prompts you to sow is the same Holy Spirit who will turn your situation around. Do you think He lacks power? Do you think He doesn't know where you're at or what you have in your bank account? He will give you power to sow *beyond your power to sow*! And He will give you the grace to rest and trust in the Lord to bring to pass that which you need.

A Place To Begin

No matter where you're at in your finances, if you haven't been operating in the anointing to sow, you need to start somewhere. In other words, don't take the attitude, *I'll step out in faith when I have more to give.*

In my meetings, I talk about obedience in giving. But I always tell people, "I didn't come here to get money from you." I don't go to those meetings to get money *from* people; I go there to teach them how to get money to come *to* them. To walk in the light of the message, they're going to have to learn giving as a way of life. They're going to have to receive the anointing to sow.

As I said, I have received that anointing, and that's why I'm enjoying financial favor and financial freedom today. I am available to God at any cost to sow any amount that He tells me to sow. And I will do it immediately. When He tells me to sow, that money is gone! Whatever the amount, I "dump it" right then and there! I know by the Word *and* by experience that whenever God tells me to give, He is setting me up to get something even bigger to me.

God can give you a sowing grace — an anointing for sowing — the results of which can surpass even the best jobs or careers. But that grace or anointing won't jump on you and overpower you. It won't even fall on you until you, first, realize that there is such a grace — and, second, until you *ask* for it.

Are You Sowing Willingly or 'Of Necessity'?

There's a grace for giving that the Church has not been properly introduced to. Instead, ministers have done just about everything else to try to get people to give. The Church at large is giving somewhat grudgingly or "of necessity" (*see* Second Corinthians 9:7).

Many people give as if they are being coerced. Someone tries to make them give by making them feel guilty — by telling them how no good they are if they don't give. Ministers will says things such as, "You're missing God if you don't give." So people feel so badly that they give just to get those ministers off their back. But when these people give, they're not giving in faith, trust, and obedience to God and His Word. They're not sowing with the expectation of harvest — that they'll reap a blessing as a result of their giving. Instead, they see what they gave simply as something they gave up and lost.

That's not what God is talking about when He tells us to give. There is an anointing in giving. There is a grace in giving, and once you act on it in faith, you begin at that very minute to head toward financial favor and financial freedom in God.

Your hands become full to overflowing — and they *stay* that way — by your receiving the grace or anointing to give beyond your power and to do it consistently. But, as I said, you have to start somewhere. You can give beyond your power where you're at right now — in your current situation.

The Sum of Your Giving

Some ministers want to talk about giving certain amounts of money as the requirement for receiving a harvest. But the Bible doesn't talk about amounts.

Let's look at something Jesus said about a certain offering one day. Jesus was watching people drop money in the offering at the temple. Rich people all around were dropping in large amounts of money. But Jesus implied that the amounts they gave were trivial in comparison to their great wealth.

Then a widow came by, who gave more than all of them even though she only gave a very small amount in comparison. Jesus commended her giving, saying, "...she of her want did cast in all that she had, even all her living" (Mark 12:44).

The Lord took special notice of this woman's giving. She got God's attention because of the grace to give that was upon her life.

Let me ask you a question. Would you rather have wealth that wasn't blessed — money that you were stingy with — or a smaller amount of wealth with a giving grace that caused God's blessing to come on what you had? When God gets finished multiplying you because of your giving, you'll be better off than the rich person who was trusting in his riches — riches that could be *here* today and completely *gone* tomorrow!

Authorized Giving

We saw in Chapter 1 that our prosperity and our right to have handfuls of plenty were paid for by Blood. Since prosperity is included in our redemption, we have been ordained and *authorized* to be blessed.

But notice that all the blessings and promises of God are conditional upon our doing something in connection or cooperation with those promises. For example, God said in Deuteronomy 28:1, "*...if thou shalt hearken diligently unto the voice of the Lord thy God, to observe and to do all his commandments which I command thee this day... the Lord thy God will set thee on high above all nations of the earth.*" Their part was the hearkening and the doing. God's part was to lift them up above the other nations.

When we do our part, God will always do His part. We start the process, or initiate it, in obedience to what He has said, and He finishes it.

Now look at Matthew 16:19 and Matthew 18:18, which say, in effect, "*Whatever you bind on earth will be bound in Heaven; and whatever you loose on earth will be loosed in Heaven.*"

You see, we have been authorized to "start something" with God. This is true in the area of finances too. If you sow a seed, God sends the harvest. You can't do His part, and He can't do your part. Receiving from God is a divine cooperation.

As we have seen in Scripture, and will continue to see, we have not only been authorized to sow, we have been *commissioned* to sow.

Is Your Seed Still In the Barn?

The prophet Haggai asks an intriguing question in Haggai 2:19.

Haggai 2:19
Is the seed yet in the barn? yea, as yet the vine, and the fig tree, and the pomegranate, and the olive tree, hath not brought forth: from this day will I bless you.

Notice this first question, "Is the seed yet in the barn?" I was meditating on that one day, and I substituted the word "bank" for the word "barn." In other words, I asked the question, "Is your seed yet in the *bank?*"

Many people have all their seed in the bank, expecting the banking system to make them rich. But some of those people are not rich toward God. In fact, they're not giving or sowing much of anything into the Kingdom of God. They might drop an occasional "five" in the offering as the bucket or plate is passed. But they aren't sowing as if God would make Heaven's resources available to them.

So many Christians today are trying to work their way to wealth just by saving. I'm not saying that saving money is wrong. I have money in the bank too. I have money invested where it can earn interest. But I don't have all my money tied up so that I can't get to it if I need to in order to give to someone else!

What I'm saying is, if all your seed is in the barn, so to speak, that means you aren't sowing any seed — you're just hoarding it.

I want you to think about that question: *Is your seed yet in the barn?* That's a powerful question. If your seed is still in the barn, there isn't going to be a harvest. How can there be a harvest when there hasn't been any sowing?

There is no harvest-producing power in the barn. But sowing

overrides hoarding, and sowing financial seed into God's Kingdom overrides the bank!

Look at the next part of Haggai 2:19: "… *as yet the vine, and the fig tree, and the pomegranate, and the olive tree, HATH NOT BROUGHT FORTH…."* No fruit comes forth when no seed has been planted — when all the seed is yet in the barn!

I remember years ago getting a small glimpse of the revelation of divine prosperity. I was convinced it was the will of God that I prosper. I desired to do the right thing with money. So I opened myself a little savings account. But it never brought forth anything for me. I was getting nowhere fast, because every time I'd put something in savings, I'd have to get it back out to pay bills. I had my meager retirement account, but I knew I was going to be retiring broke if I didn't sow as the Lord led me to sow.

Can you relate to that? I had to get to a place where I could say, "All right, Lord, whatever You say to do with my money, that's what I'll do."

You, too, will have to get to the point where the anointing of God has taken you over, and you are just watching and waiting to do whatever God says to do with your money.

The Crucial Role of Sowing

I alluded to this earlier in the chapter, but it bears repeating: Your harvest level will not change until your sowing level changes first. Many people want to change their harvest, yet they are not changing their seed. I believe in prayer, praise, and the confession, or profession, of God's Word for finances. But all of that won't work without sowing financial seed.

Many people want to emphasize prayer, claiming that a breakthrough in prayer will help their financial condition. But when they get done praying about their harvest, the Lord still says, "Let's talk about a seed."

Other people claim that praise is the way to financial victory. But when you get done *praising,* you're going to have to come back to the *principle!*

Friend, if you want out of your financial situation, you're going to have to sow your way out — not work your way out, pray your way out, praise your way out, meditate your way out, and so forth. Harvest comes from planting seed. What you sow is what you're going to reap (*see* Galatians 6:9).

Friend, there is no substitute for sowing. Where there is famine, limitation, and lack, there can come a revelation — truth from God's Word — that if acted upon in faith can cause an outpouring of abundance. "Anointed sowing" is one of those outstanding truths.

CHAPTER FIVE

The Power of Hands That Are Anointed To Sow!

We've established the fact that God wants to put something in your hands to sow in order to activate His principles, plans, and promises in your life. When your hands are anointed to sow, you prove out these principles and you cooperate with God to see that His covenant is established in your life.

From God's point of view, you're already blessed. Jesus paid the full price in His death, burial, and resurrection for our redemption, which includes financial freedom. But the world and the enemy of your soul, Satan, will try to keep you from realizing or enjoying that freedom. However, God has made a way for their plans to be frustrated — through your faith and obedience to Him. When you cooperate with God by allowing Him to put something in your hands to sow and by sowing it in obedience to

Him, you give God the right to do something extraordinary in your life.

When these truths sink deep into your heart and mind, you will realize the great truth that your own hands can tie or loose God's hands on your behalf.

The Heart and Hand Connection

Your hands can't be anointed to sow until your heart and mind are anointed to sow. In other words, the Word of God concerning giving and receiving, or sowing and reaping, is going to have to be planted deeply in your heart. Otherwise, God will prompt you to sow the biggest seed you've ever sown, and your mind will react to that, saying, *"What! That's my grocery money!"*

Your mind will go "tilt," and you'll think you're losing your mind! In other words, you will react naturally instead of spiritually, because you haven't understood some things correctly, and you haven't settled some things in your heart.

For example, if you have a mortgage payment or a utility bill that's due, and God says to you, *"Put that money in the offering,"* you might do it, but your mind hits afterward, *Why did I do that!*

You have to get the Word settled in your heart and mind, because when your heart and mind become anointed to sow, your hands will be anointed too. You will obey willingly and sow with great joy and expectation, because you know that "Money Cometh" and that your harvest is on its way!

Qualified Reaping

Some people say, "I'm just believing God's Word for my prosperity. He meets all of my needs according to His riches in glory by Christ Jesus." They are quoting Philippians 4:19, but if you read that verse in its context, you will see that Paul was talking about sowing and reaping. The people in that Philippian church were big givers. Their hands were anointed to sow, and that's why they could claim their every need supplied by the resources of Heaven.

So, you see, walking in divine prosperity is more than believing the Word. It's acting on the truths of God's Word, the principles of the Bible, that causes you to enter the realm of plenty. As I said, you can shout, dance, and praise God all you want — and you can pray in tongues all you want — but there will come a time when you will have to act on your faith and your believing by sowing an anointed seed.

The Difference Between Marketing and the Anointing (There's a Big Difference!)

In the last chapter, I said that many Christians are giving without a revelation and with the anointing because they feel coerced to give. They're not willingly obeying any unction from the Spirit of God to give because they don't have the Word of God in their heart on the subject. Their hands have not been anointed to sow.

When I encourage people to sow by the unction, I am not talking about sowing under compunction! I'm not talking about getting all worked up over someone on TV who wants to send you a special scarf, special oil, or "holy water" in return for an offering!

Numerous people have approached me about marketing "Money Cometh" as a slogan on handkerchiefs, T-shirts, license plates, pens, pencils, and so forth. But the Holy Spirit said to me, "Don't ever merchandise this revelation." If you know anything about me, you know that I don't even have a song or chorus in my church about "Money Cometh."

I'm not against marketing per se, because it can be a valuable tool, and we should not overlook it. But in my case, the Lord never told me to sell "Money Cometh" as a commodity; He told me to teach it as a *revelation*. And putting that saying on common items such as a handkerchief or T-shirt lowers the revelation and the dignity of the message. "Money Cometh" loses some of its sanctity when you cheapen it by marketing it with a trinket.

I've said many times before that "Money Cometh" is not a fad. It's a holy saying that will be here until Jesus comes back. There is an anointing on "Money Cometh" and on the revelation of divine prosperity that God has commissioned me to teach. It's my assignment, and there is an anointing that goes with it. I will not do anything to tamper with that anointing.

'Money Cometh' and the Anointing To Sow

In previous chapters, we looked at the fact that the anointing and money do go together at times — times when God is blessing a person or a group of people financially. Let me show you something else about "Money Cometh" in connection with anointed sowing or hands that are anointed to sow.

Years ago, when I first received the revelation of "Money Cometh," I was in Virginia in a meeting, and a man there told me about a verse he'd found that had the words "money cometh" in it. Now, I don't "jump," or act, every time someone shows me something. I just let what's said sort of incubate in my spirit so I can hear what the Lord is saying about it.

I listened to what this man had to say, and he showed me Second Kings 12:4.

2 Kings 12:4-5
4 And Jehoash said to the priests, All the money of the dedicated things that is brought into the house of the

Lord, even the money of every one that passeth the account, the money that every man is set at, and all the MONEY THAT COMETH into any man's heart to bring into the house of the Lord,
5 Let the priests take it to them, every man of his acquaintance: and let them repair the breaches of the house, wheresoever any breach shall be found.

These verses are talking about voluntary offerings — *"money that cometh* into any man's heart to bring" — that the priests were receiving to repair the house of the Lord. I want to show you some things from verse 4 that are profound and that contain enough revelation to set you financially free — and *swiftly* — if you get hold of it in your heart.

First, we know that anointed sowing is an issue of the heart. Hands that are anointed to sow are anointed because the heart and mind were anointed first. The heart and mind were heavy with revelation knowledge from the Word that prompted the hands to give.

People have thought that the revelation of "Money Cometh" would work just by their saying it over and over again. Certainly, you have to speak forth that which you believe. There is a real truth that unites believing and speaking (2 Corinthians 4:13). However, just as Jehoash said to collect *"...the money that cometh into any man's heart to bring...,"* the revelation of "Money Cometh" must come to your heart first before it can benefit you or others. But when you get it in your heart, you'll say concerning giving, "Let's bring it!" And God will "bring it" back to you!

Why Do People Bring Money to the Altar?

The first time I preached on "Money Cometh" years ago, I was in a certain city ministering in a large auditorium. As I was ministering, at one point, people just started running toward the altar in droves, dropping money at my feet as I ministered. I was shocked — it was the first time I'd seen anything like that.

When these people jumped up and started running, at first I didn't know what they were doing or where they were headed. I didn't act scared or shocked. I had to look calm, like I knew what I was doing, since I was in charge of the service! But I honestly didn't know what was going on. I thought that maybe the people were running to the altar to get saved. I thought, *Well, I thought I was preaching about prosperity, but maybe I preached something about Heaven!*

Then I saw that the people running had money in their hands. I came to recognize that what was happening was a result of the anointing that comes upon people when they get a revelation in their heart. These people's hearts and hands had become anointed to sow, and they had to sow!

This has happened many times since that day. It began an ongoing process by which God is setting up the Body of Christ for their ongoing harvest.

'Set' In Your Giving — 'Stuck' In Your Receiving

2 Kings 12:4
And Jehoash said to the priests, All the money of the dedicated things that is brought into the house of the Lord, even the money of every one that passeth the account, THE MONEY THAT EVERY MAN IS SET AT, and all the money that cometh into any man's heart to bring into the house of the Lord.

Notice the phrase, "*...the money that every man IS SET at....*" I like the way that reads in the *King James Version*. This phrase was referring to every man giving according to his assessment at the census. Then beyond his assessment, or the amount he was "set" at, he would give according to *"...the money that cometh..."* into his heart.

Some people today have giving accounts, or amounts they have set aside and have predetermined to give to the Lord beyond their tithe. That's a good thing, as long as they're open to the Spirit of God when He tells them to go over and beyond what they've set aside to give. If they're not open, then they've become "set" in their giving. When you become *set* in your giving, you become *stuck* in your receiving.

Some people are set at "five-dollar" giving. I know that because many years ago, I was set on "five" in the Baptist church I attended. I didn't *tithe* and I was set at *five!* I didn't care what that pastor preached on — I was *set!*

Some people are like that today. Some will even stay away from prosperity meetings because they see them as nothing more than "the-man-of-God-wants-me-to-give-something meetings." If they do attend, they have the attitude, *"I don't care if a four-winged angel comes and sits down in front of me and stares me down eyeball to eyeball — I'm not giving a dime!"*

There are many reasons why people become "set" in their giving. Some are blinded to God's Word, and doubt and unbelief hold them back because they won't open their heart or mind to consider the truth. Others have seen too much abuse with money in the Body of Christ, so they close themselves off from the truth — from what's real and genuine. And others are just plain stingy!

Whatever the reason, they can choose to hear the Word of God with hearing ears and receive the anointing to sow. As I said, that sowing anointing is a divine enabling to give; it's a giving, or sowing, grace. And once the Lord gives you a sowing anointing, you won't have trouble anymore with thoughts that someone is trying to rob you from the pulpit. (There have been preachers who've "robbed" people, because those preachers were looking to man to meet their needs; they weren't trusting God.)

When your heart is set on giving and you have hands anointed for sowing, you'll know the real thing when you see it. You'll know that you're dealing with God and not with any man. Your sowing becomes a matter between you and God — and your reaping becomes a matter between you and God, a matter that God will take into His own hands because your hands became anointed to sow!

The Power of the Seed Sown

It's important never to underestimate the power of hands that have been anointed to sow. It's also important never to underestimate the power of the seed that is sown. The content of your harvest is contained within your seed.

A woman who has followed my ministry for years recently wrote me a nice letter and sent me a $10,000 check. In her letter, she related that sending that $10,000 was as easy as sending $10 years ago when she first began seeing the revelation of divine prosperity, or of prospering God's way and by His hand. This woman's hands are anointed to sow. She has the Word in her heart and has been acting on that Word in faith and obedience for some time.

And the revelation is producing a harvest in her life. The anointing is working for her. But she started where she was at — with the $10 seed. When she received the Word of God, she began acting on it right then. She didn't take the attitude, *I'll just wait until I have more to give.* She esteemed the Word of God, and she esteemed her seed. She saw the power in her seed, and she released that power by sowing it.

Finally, at the bottom of this woman's letter, in her closing, she wrote the words: *Flourishing with no lack and no limitation.*

How did she do it? She asked God for the anointing to sow and she applied herself to the study of God's Word concerning finances. She overpowered lack and limitations with the principles of God's Word.

That is what the anointing to sow is doing for this woman, and that is exactly what it will do for you. God will anoint you and give you sowing hands, but He has to begin in your heart. He will anoint your heart first, and then it will get in your hands. When you have a heart for sowing, your hands will be blessed. Every time you reach out your hands to sow, you're sowing a blessing, and those same hands will be anointed to *receive* a blessing too!

Wealthy and Sad — You Can Have Wealth In Your Hands and Leanness In Your Heart

I want to show you the power of sowing from a heart that's willing to give because it is fully turned toward the Lord. But I also want you to see the tragedy of a heart that's *not* fully committed.

Mark 10:17-24
17 And when he was gone forth into the way, there came one running, and kneeled to him, and asked him, Good Master, what shall I do that I may inherit eternal life?
18 And Jesus said unto him, Why callest thou me good? there is none good but one, that is, God.
19 Thou knowest the commandments, Do not commit adultery, Do not kill, Do not steal, Do not bear false witness, Defraud not, Honour thy father and mother.
20 And he answered and said unto him, Master, all these have I observed from my youth.

21 Then Jesus beholding him loved him, and said unto him, One thing thou lackest: go thy way, sell whatsoever thou hast, and give to the poor, and thou shalt have treasure in heaven: and come, take up the cross, and follow me.

22 And he was sad at that saying, and went away grieved: for he had great possessions.

23 And Jesus looked round about, and saith unto his disciples, How hardly shall they that have riches enter into the kingdom of God!

24 And the disciples were astonished at his words. But Jesus answereth again, and saith unto them, Children, how hard is it for them that TRUST IN RICHES to enter into the kingdom of God!

In this passage, Jesus was dealing with a rich young ruler, who was a religious man. This boy had been talking about all of his religious "acrobats" and deeds, and it says that afterward, *"...Jesus beholding him loved him, and said unto him, One thing thou lackest: go thy way, sell whatsoever thou hast, and give to the poor, and thou shalt have treasure in heaven: and come, take up the cross, and follow me"* (verse 21).

Jesus had to go to the extreme with this boy because money had him hooked. It's not for everyone to do what Jesus instructed this young man to do, but Jesus knew He had to get the man unhooked from money before he could follow Him and give his heart to the Lord completely.

Verse 22 says the young ruler, *"...was sad at that saying, and went away grieved [or sad]: for he had great possessions."*

I see this same emotion among many in the Church who have some material wealth. Possessions and the desire for more possessions dominate their thinking. The Lord doesn't really have a place in their hearts and minds because they are too focused on their money. They have some wealth in their hands, but they have leanness in their hearts. Therefore, their hands are not anointed to sow.

Unless these people make some changes, they will never know the joy of cooperating with God's bigger plan to bless them and to make them a blessing to others. Instead, all they'll know is the daily, grinding task of obsessing over money, and the desperation that will beset them if something should happen to the money they're trusting in so heavily.

Don't you know that's why the Lord tests individuals and builds their character as they're walking by faith and sowing their seed? Have you ever seen television programs about people who win the lottery? Most of those people end up completely ruined and broke. God doesn't want to see that happen to you as His child when your financial captivity is turned. That's why you have to have a revelation in your heart and the anointing on your hands. It will cause you to give by faith, trusting in the Lord, not on your money or even on your giving. There will be some character and some steadfastness attached to your sowing that will cause you to increase and to *abide* in financial wealth.

As we will see in the following chapters, God sets us up to go through our seasons of patient waiting and of developing in character as a means of preparing us for what He already knows He's going to do. Our job is to stay faithful to His Word, consistent in our sowing, and in a constant state of expectancy so that we don't lose heart. He is faithful who promised (Hebrews 10:23)!

Sow With Your Hands or 'Water With Your Foot'!

Remember I said at the beginning of this chapter that your own hands can tie or loose God's hands on your behalf God. Your sowing enables God to work behind the scenes on your behalf so He can unveil your harvest when they time is right.

But God wants you to sow without struggles — without doubting and despairing. He wants you to sow with grace and peace, knowing that He is up to something big on your behalf.

In referring to the land of Canaan, the Israelites' promised land, the Lord repeatedly described to Moses and the children of Israel the thing He was "up to" on their behalf.

The following is just one of many such descriptions.

Deuteronomy 11:10-12
10 For the land, whither thou goest in to possess it, is not as the land of Egypt, from whence ye came out, where thou sowedst thy seed, and wateredst it with thy foot, as a garden of herbs:
11 But the land, whither ye go to possess it, is a land of hills and valleys, and drinketh water of the rain of heaven:
12 A land which the Lord thy God careth for: the eyes of the Lord thy God are always upon it, from the beginning of the year even unto the end of the year.

In verses 10 and 11, there is a great shift for the children of Israel: "*For the land, whither thou goest in to possess it, IS NOT AS THE LAND OF EGYPT, from whence ye came out, WHERE THOU SOWEDST THY SEED, AND WATEREDST IT WITH THY FOOT, as a garden of herbs: But the land, whither ye go to possess it, IS A LAND OF HILLS AND VALLEYS, AND DRINKETH WATER OF THE RAIN OF HEAVEN."*

God's people had lived in slavery in Egypt and had been supernaturally delivered and provided with great wealth. Now God was trying to bring them into their own land, where they could settle. This new land was nothing like where they'd lived in Egypt.

The children of Israel had worked hard as slaves, performing work that was physically and mentally exhausting with nothing to show for it at the end of each long day. God was showing them something new. Whereas His people had "watered with their feet" the land in Egypt where they'd toiled, this new land was a land that was rich and fertile, a land that God Himself would water and bless.

People in the Body of Christ today have been watering with their feet for too long, expecting their job to provide for them everything they need. But God wants to add His blessing and add so much quality of life to each one of His children. There is a land you can enter through your faith, trust, and obedience that God Himself will care for! Notice you'll continue to sow seed in this new "land." But God will water it Himself and bring forth multiplied blessings that you have not experienced before now.

Dare to believe in God's goodness and that every one of His promises is true. Don't be one of those people who refuses to sow with his hands, and just continues day after day to "water with his feet," working hard but not getting very far in life. There's harvest-producing power in your hands when you're willing to sow a seed!

Stewardship: The Faith and Obedience Connection

Do you want full hands — hands that are filled with divine prosperity? If you do, you're going to have to develop hands that are yielded to God so that He can anoint them for sowing. In other words, developing in stewardship is a requirement of the Lord you must meet so He can permit your hands to have a continuously full supply.

What Will You Do With What God Places in Your Hands?

Stewardship is the ability to manage something. So you are going to have to prove your ability to manage the money God gives you so that He can give you more. You will begin with a certain amount, but you can end up with an amount that is beyond your comprehension today.

Obedience: The Key to Miracles

Obedience is the key to miracles. Have you ever read the verse, *"...Whatsoever he saith unto you, do it"* (John 2:5)? At the wedding at Cana, the bride and groom ran out of wine to serve their guests. Mary, the mother of Jesus, said to Jesus, "Do something." Then she looked at the servants and told them, "Whatever my son tells you to do, *do it!"* You know what happened next. The first of Jesus' public miracles occurred that day as water pot after water pot was filled with water and then miraculously touched by the hand of God to become wine. (*See* John 2:1-11.)

How could water become wine without some supernatural touch upon it? And what could a rod do to part the mighty waters of the Red Sea? Yet God commanded Moses to stretch forth his rod, and by Moses' obedience, God delivered millions of people from a fierce army in hot pursuit. God's people marched across that sea on dry land (*see* Exodus 14:10-31)!

And what does shouting have to do with crumbling a fortified city as impenetrable as Jericho? Yet when God told Joshua to instruct the people to march around that city's walls once a day for six days. Then on the seventh day, they were to march around that place seven times and then to shout after the blowing of the trumpets. Joshua obeyed — and so did the people — and those concrete walls came crashing down (*see* Joshua chapter 6).

In much the same way, when God tells you to do something, *do it!* Or if He tells a man or woman of God how to instruct you, show respect for that anointed vessel and obey the word of the Lord as if you were obeying the Lord Himself. Remember, Second Chronicles 20:20 says, *"...Believe in the Lord your God, so shall ye be established; believe his prophets, so shall ye prosper."*

Why Stewardship?

I said in a previous chapter that someone must pay for the work of God to go forward. If stewards of God don't pay for the work of God, then the work of God will be hindered or even left undone until other stewards pick up the baton, so to speak, and carry forth God's will in the earth where others were unwilling.

Believers are to be God's stewards for a twofold purpose. First, God needs to have His work financed. Second, God knows He can't bless you like He wants to unless you sow the right seed. He knows that He has to supply seed to the sower before the sower can become an eater (*see* Isaiah 55:10). Yet how many times has He entrusted a degree of wealth to stewards who then wasted every dime on themselves and forgot to sow. They tied God's hands so that He couldn't continue blessing them like He wanted to.

When God makes a financial deposit into your life, He expects you to be His treasurer so that He can call on you anytime to give what He wants you to give. In so doing, He always gives you enough to enjoy life with. You may not start out where you want to be. You must begin with an understanding of God's purposes for money and with a heart to trust and obey. If God sees that your purposes are aligned with His purposes and that He can steer and anoint your hands to sow, He will increase you.

We established the truth that God does not want you empty-handed — without any seed to sow and without any harvest or abundant provision as a result of your sowing. When your hands are full of God's provision, you have enough for your needs, desires, and dreams. But remember, full *hands* are an indication of a full *heart* — of a heart and mind full of revelation knowledge from God's Word concerning His purposes for money.

In other words, when your hands and heart are full because God filled them, you won't spend everything you get on just you and yours. You will help others, and you will do it regularly as a steward of the finances God has entrusted to you.

Stewardship Begins With the Tithe

As a Baptist boy preacher, although I was ignorant of God's Word concerning wealth, the passage in Matthew 25:14-30 always intrigued me. I knew that there was more in it than I'd ever heard preached by my pastor or by any radio or television preacher. I knew there was more in there, but I just couldn't put my finger on it, so to speak.

Let's look at two of those verses in that passage.

Matthew 25:14-15
14 For the kingdom of heaven is as a man travelling into a far country, who called his own servants, and delivered unto them his goods.
15 And unto one he gave five talents, to another two, and to another one; to every man according to his several ability; and straightway took his journey.

This passage is talking about stewardship. The goods that were placed in each of those servants' hands came from God, and, in reality, belonged to God. The same is true for us today.

Bugged by the 'Bug Man'

I remember the first time I began to fully recognize that fact. Actually, it was when I first began to think about tithing. I was a young Baptist preacher, and I knew a little about tithing. I knew that other people tithed, but I didn't tithe.

I often tell the following story to make a crucial point

concerning the message of prosperity. One day, the exterminator was at our Baptist church spraying for bugs. (In south Louisiana, we call him the "roach man," because with all the humidity we have down here, water roaches are our number-one insect problem.) After he was done, he wrote up an invoice for the work he'd done. Underneath the total, he wrote the words, "Less ten percent."

Back then, I only had one person working for me, so I handled a lot of the church's business myself. I looked at the man's bill to approve it before asking my secretary to write a check. I saw the words, "Less ten percent" and asked him, "So you're doing a favor for the church?"

The man answered, in effect, "No, not exactly. It's not a favor. I'm a tither, so I tithe off all of my work."

Now, the tithe means *the tenth*. So the roach man was saying that he gave ten percent of all his income.

Now I was the pastor, and I *wasn't* a tither! How do you think I felt when he said that? I tried to shake it off. After the man left, I got in my car to go visit a fellow minister, and I turned the radio on really loud to try to drown out those words, *I'm a tither*, that seemed to echo in my head.

My radio dial was set to a station that aired Christian teaching, and a man's voice came over the airwaves talking about the tithe! I changed stations fast!

Then I arrived at my friend's house. I just knew *he* wouldn't be talking about the tithe. He was a Baptist preacher, too, who'd been teaching longer than I had. I knew I'd be safe with him, because back then, it seemed that most of the Baptists I knew were tight-fisted! We Baptists never talked much about tithing.

We hadn't gotten but about three or four minutes into our conversation when my friend said, "Leroy, are you a tither?"

What! I knew right then that all "hell" had broken loose!

Actually, it was *Heaven* breaking loose on me, trying to get me out from under hell's jurisdiction in the realm of finances.

I made my mind right then and there to become a tither. In fact, I called my wife and said to her, "From now on, everything that comes into our house, we're going to give ten percent of it to the Lord."

We just did it. We didn't *prepare* to do it; we just acted immediately one day on the truth of the tithe. We were broker than the Ten Commandments coming down from Mount Sinai! I mean, we had bills up to our grandkids' necks (and we didn't even have grandchildren at the time)! But we paid our tithes from that day forth. We put God first. We paid the tithe, the *tenth*, first before any of our bills.

You see, the tithe is not a seed you *sow*; the tithe is something you *owe*. The Word says that the tithe belongs to God (*see* Leviticus 27:30 *NIV*) and that a man (or woman) robs God when he withholds the tithe (Malachi 3:8).

The Blessing of Obedience

Well, we were tithers for years without seeing any significant result. But we were happy because we knew tithing was the right thing to do, and we were being obedient. I'm sure God protected us from a lot of things that could have hurt us financially. (You see, there is a blessing in obedience that we haven't fully realized. And there's a certain happiness that comes in obeying the will of God for your life.)

As Carolyn and I kept on tithing, we continued receiving more and more revelation on the subject of divine prosperity as we went along. When you're walking in the light of what you know, you'll receive more light.

I shared that to illustrate to you that you can't even begin to be a steward of finances if you're not tithing. After you've paid what you owe — your tithe — *then* you can successfully manage, as a sower, the wealth or increase that God places in your hands. Stewardship begins with the tithe.

Are You a Money-Manager For God?

Matthew 25:15 says, *"And unto one he gave five talents, to another two, and to another one; to every man ACCORDING TO HIS SEVERAL ABILITY; and straightway took his journey."*

Look at the phrase, *"...according to his several ability...."* Here is what that phrase boils down to: *According to your personal ability to manage Kingdom resources, that's how much you're going to have placed by God into your hands.*

Now let's look at what happened when the master, who had distributed the talents, returned from his journey.

Matthew 25:19-28
19 After a long time the lord of those servants cometh, and reckoneth with them.
20 And so he that had received five talents came and brought other five talents, saying, Lord, thou deliveredst unto me five talents: behold, I have gained beside them five talents more.
21 His lord said unto him, Well done, thou good and faithful servant: thou hast been faithful over a few things, I will make thee ruler over many things: enter thou into the joy of thy lord.
22 He also that had received two talents came and said, Lord, thou deliveredst unto me two talents: behold, I have gained two other talents beside them.
23 His lord said unto him, Well done, good and faithful servant; thou hast been faithful over a few things, I will

make thee ruler over many things: enter thou into the joy of thy lord.

24 Then he which had received the one talent came and said, Lord, I knew thee that thou art an hard man, reaping where thou hast not sown, and gathering where thou hast not strawed:

25 And I was afraid, and went and hid thy talent in the earth: lo, there thou hast that is thine.

26 His lord answered and said unto him, Thou wicked and slothful servant, thou knewest that I reap where I sowed not, and gather where I have not strawed:

27 Thou oughtest therefore to have put my money to the exchangers, and then at my coming I should have received mine own with usury.

28 Take therefore the talent from him, and give it unto him which hath ten talents.

Verse 19 says, *"After a long time the lord of those servants cometh, and reckoneth with them."* The *New King James Version* says, "After a long time the lord of those servants came and *settled accounts* with them."

The Lord will check on your stewardship. He is watching what you do with your life, and He is watching what you do with money.

Are You Ready For Wealth?

Have you ever known someone who received a lump sum of money and just went crazy with it? They spent it so fast — then they had nothing to show for the wealth that was entrusted to them.

Other people will receive a "lump sum" and hold on to it so tight that they become obsessed with it. I know a woman whose husband died and left her some money. Both the husband and wife were members of my church. After the woman received her money, she shunned me and the church. I didn't want her money, but I guess she thought I did, because anytime she saw me in public, she would duck and hide so she wouldn't have to see me.

That woman died shortly afterward. Maybe she worried about that money too much. Whatever the case, she became preoccupied with money. It wasn't very much money, yet it drove her from the path God had set before her, because she was so obsessed with it that she thought everyone was after it.

You can keep increase from coming to you by holding on too tight to what you have. This is true even in the natural. For example, if you're so concerned about your money that you keep going back to the bank every couple of days to withdraw it, you are "choking" that money and holding it back from increasing!

If you're not anointed for money — if you're not an anointed sower — you will want to see your money every five minutes. You're trusting in that money, but deep down, you know it's not trustworthy. You know it could be gone as fast as you got it. So you obsess over it.

One time, I had a word from God for a young woman whose mother Carolyn and I knew well. This young woman was the wife of a professional athlete. The two of them had money, but they didn't have principles; they had no principles in place to live by in the area of finances. I knew the Lord was dealing with them about seeking His face and about getting some things right with Him. I saw this woman one day in front of a certain store, and I spoke to her about what I sensed the Lord was trying to get across to them. I actually sensed something strange was about to happen if they didn't make some changes.

When I related to her everything the Lord told me to say, I

could tell she didn't receive it. Maybe she thought I wanted something from her. I only wanted to equip them so that it would go well with them for a long, long time. I didn't want them to get so caught up in the pleasures of "right now" that they missed what God was telling them to do that would set them up securely for the rest of their lives.

The woman didn't receive what I told her. Now the couple is divorced, and most of their money is gone. If she had listened to me that day in front of that store, their situation could have turned out differently.

In another case, a certain couple's son was a superstar in high school. The Lord spoke to me to visit this family. College scouts were looking at this boy, and I felt the Lord actually prompt me about what school He wanted the young man to attend.

So I obeyed the Lord and shared with them what I sensed He wanted me to say. I think the woman thought I was trying to get her son to attend a school near our church so she would join our church, because the first thing out of her mouth was, "I'm not leaving my church." She thought I was trying to recruit her, but I was trying to rescue her.

That was years ago, and today that young man is doing some kind of insignificant work even though he had greatness in his future. He missed the whole flow. He found out he wasn't as good as he thought he was without the Lord.

I'm talking about those who missed it with wealth because they weren't rich toward God (*see* Luke 12:21). But there are many today who *aren't* missing it with their money. They are acting as good stewards of the finances God has entrusted to them, and they are being blessed as a result.

For example, I have had members of my church receive large sums of money and call the church during the week, saying, in effect, "I have to come over right now and pay my tithe, or this money is going to crush me!"

That's good stewardship. Remember, I said that you can't even begin to sow until you've paid what you owe. And we all owe the Lord the tithe, or the tenth, of our increase.

Part of my job is to guide people to enter into a divine flow, a divine cooperation, with the Lord so that He can give them increase, just as the master did with the servants in the Parable of the Talents. But some people just won't listen to the truth.

Because teaching divine prosperity is my assignment from Heaven, I face people all the time who have misgivings about my motives. But I'm already rich; I am already a multi-millionaire. And I don't have any debt. I don't need their money; I'm simply trying to help them by teaching them the things the Lord has taught me.

Some people get offended because I talk so much about what I have. I am living in my dream home. It's a mansion, and it's paid for. I have several automobiles. They're nice cars, and they're paid for. My wife and I wear nice clothing. We live in the best, drive the best, wear the best, and eat the best (*see* Isaiah 1:19). I don't talk about all that to brag; I do it to teach. The things I teach others are things I have practiced and experienced for myself.

I'm not bragging about my status, but I am bragging on God. The wealth I enjoy today came through my obeying the same principles that I teach others.

Actually, I received my breakthrough years ago. I have been rich for a while! Since then, I've learned so much more, and now I'm able to teach even more truths and greater principles than I knew back when I first broke through the wall of poverty that loomed high over my life. How much more should you receive your breakthrough today!

Three Stages of Stewardship

I see three stages of stewardship in the passage in Matthew chapter 25, in the Parable of the Talents. *First*, God gives you a certain amount of money to steward, or manage, for Him. *Second,* God checks your faith as He "settles your account." In other words, did you have enough faith to sow and believe that He would multiply your seed sown (2 Corinthians 9:10)? *Third,* if you pass the test and show Him some faith, trust, and obedience, He promotes you in the realm of finances.

Here are the three stages:

1. God gives you seed according to your ability to handle Kingdom resources (Matthew 25:14-15).

2. God tests you with a few things first and increases you by how faithful He finds you in the "little" (verses 16-19).

3. When God finds you faithful with the resources He gives you, He changes your status, and you go from faithful to ruler (verses 20-23).

When you become a ruler over the finances God gives you, you no longer need to be tested. You enter into the joy of the Lord, where the resources of God are at your disposal. You move from *supply* to *surplus* — from God supplying your needs to God putting into your hands money far beyond that which you need.

From Manager to Master —
Lessons From the Faithful Steward

Matthew 25:21 says to the faithful steward, "*…Well done, thou good and faithful servant: thou hast been faithful over a few things, I will make thee ruler over many things: enter thou into the joy of thy lord.*"

There is a divine method and a divine flow to experiencing financial increase in God's Kingdom. For example, the wise stewards in the Parable of the Talents went from managers to masters — from being "faithful" over little to being "rulers" over much.

Being faithful and being a ruler are two different things. When I am being faithful, it is for someone else. When I become a ruler, I have the dominion. In the case of money, God can trust me with more money than just a little to be faithful with, because He knows I will sow where He wants me to sow every time and that I will be instantly obedient. I will move according to His beck and call whether I'm hurting or happy. He knows money is not going to take His place with me, because He is my first love. So He lets me rule over greater and greater amounts.

Did you know that one test as to whether God is your first love is the giving test? In other words, you prove that God is first by your giving.

From *Testing* to *Trusting*

When God proves you in the "little" — with the few things — it is called *testing*. When He proves you with the "much" — with the many things — it is called *trusting*. You want to be at the place of trusting, where God trusts you with untold amounts, because you will do the right thing with money.

Every time God tells you to give something, He is trying to get something better to you. God doesn't want you to be a "squeezer" — someone who gets hold of money and squeezes it so tight it can't breathe! Money has to keep flowing in order for God to keep blessing you. If your money doesn't flow, nothing can flow back to you.

In other words, you have to keep money alive. Money stagnates when you pursue it and pocket it! You have to keep money alive by sowing it.

I'm talking about a divine way of doing things, not a natural, worldly way. The world lives big as if the Body of Christ isn't allowed to live big. But the devil is a liar. Jesus is the

Messiah. He is the Faithful and True Witness, the Word of God that was made flesh and that dwelt among us (Revelation 3:14; John 1:14). He paid a great price to set us free from poverty and lack.

Why do so many Christians act as if the world has all the expertise where money is concerned? They get all excited over Hollywood actors and professional athletes and their houses, cars, and clothes — when they should be getting excited about the Word of God, which can make them wealthy too!

We should be trusting God to make us rulers over finances because of our faithfulness. Then we can enjoy enduring riches without have to trust in this world's system, which can let us down flat on our backs in a minute's time. But when we are faithful rulers over finances because we got there *God's* way, finances will not rule over us. We will not be high-minded, trusting in those riches. Instead, we will be trusting in the Living God, who gave us those riches. (*See* First Timothy 6:17.)

Some believers think they're ruling over finances just because they're making ends meet and enjoying a little more besides. But finances are ruling over you if you're working a job you don't like, if you're working overtime to have the things you need or want, if you're working more than one job, if you carry a credit-card balance each month, and so forth.

Friend, that's not financial dominion. That is not God's plan. Don't be satisfied with less than God's best for your life. You can allow God to promote you from being faithful to being a ruler, someone who *dominates* finances and has authority where money is concerned.

It's Time For Your 'Afterward'!

Do you hold a promise of God in your heart as dear? Are you looking with confidence toward a manifestation of financial favor in your life? Just as God created an expectation in the hearts of His people in the Old Testament of their deliverance from Egyptian slavery, He will create an expectation in your heart of your financial freedom from captivity. You may be going through something that's unpleasant or painful today, but God wants to show you your "afterward."

Genesis 15:13-14
13 And he said unto Abram, Know of a surety that thy seed shall be a stranger in a land that is not theirs, and

shall serve them; and they shall afflict them four hundred years;
14 And also that nation, whom they shall serve, will I judge: and AFTERWARD SHALL THEY COME OUT WITH GREAT SUBSTANCE.

God was speaking to Abram (whose name was later changed to Abraham) about the future captivity of the Israelites. But many in the Body of Christ have been in captivity too — in financial captivity. Their captivity is due to ignorance of their freedom in Christ and of their covenant with God.

A Promise Made and a Promise Kept

Let's look again at the passage in Genesis 15: *"And he said unto Abram, Know of a surety that thy seed shall be a stranger in a land that is not theirs, and shall serve them; and they shall afflict them four hundred years; And also that nation, whom they shall serve, will I judge: and afterward shall they come out with great substance."*

Notice the promise God made to the natural seed, or descendants, of Abraham. He said, in effect, that after they were delivered from their captivity, they would come out *with great abundance* (v. 14).

Now, when I see a promise in the Bible, I gravitate toward it and pay attention, because most of the Bible promises belong to me as a Christian, as a child of the Most High God. Hebrews 8:6 says that our promises as New Testament believers are even better: *"But now hath he [Jesus] obtained a more excellent ministry, by how much also he is the mediator of A BETTER COVENANT, which was established upon BETTER PROMISES."*

Those under the Old Covenant weren't under the blood of Jesus yet. But we who have accepted Him as Savior are under His blood and are qualified to partake of the blessings of the New Covenant.

Notice that after God told Abram that his people would one day be in captivity for 400 years, God promised His covenant friend, *"And also that nation, whom they shall serve, will I judge: and AFTERWARD shall they come out with great substance"* (Genesis 15:14).

I believe that we in the Body of Christ are in the "afterward"! We are coming out of financial captivity. Notice that verse doesn't just say the Israelites came out of their captivity with substance. It says they came out with *great* substance!

Know 'of a Surety' and Rejoice In Your 'Afterward'

Now let's look at that phrase, *"...Know of a surety..."* (v. 13). When the Holy Ghost breathes out the words, "Know of a surety," you can bank on one hundred percent of what follows to come to pass. Therefore, we can read verses 13 and 14 and conclude that Abram knew *of a surety* that his people would one day be strangers and slaves in a land not their own (v. 13). He knew *of a surety* that they would be afflicted for 400 years (v. 13). He knew *of a surety* that God would judge the nation that took them captive (v. 14). And, finally, Abram knew *of a surety* that they *would come OUT OF CAPTIVITY WITH GREAT ABUNDANCE* (v. 14)!

It's Time For Your 'Afterward'!

God foretold the adversity that would befall the natural descendants of Abraham, but God didn't leave Abraham hanging with news of captivity, doom, and gloom. No, God left Abraham with a promise of "afterward." And God will always promise you an "afterward" too.

We have focused too much on our tests and trials and our captivities. Instead, we need to begin to dance like it's our "afterward"!

Some people are still sitting down in the ashes of their "before." In fact, some of them seem glued to their ashes! They are clinging to what happened in the past. But your life does not have to consist of just "more of the same." God's promises are *yes* and *amen* in Christ Jesus (2 Corinthians 1:20). Those promises are "*right-now*" promises for those who will take them by faith and set their face like flint, expecting an answer! (*See* Isaiah 50:7.)

So what is your financial "afterward"? It can be different things for different people, depending on where each one is at in his finances. For example, the following scenarios describe some "afterward" situations.

"*After* I suffered leanness and lack all these years, I am now walking in the realm of plenty!"

"*After* I worked three jobs to try to make it, I learned God's principles of prosperity. I now live by principles instead of by my job, and I am rich!"

"*After* I lost everything, God has restored me, and I have twice as much as I had before, plus I have the knowledge that He is indeed a covenant-keeping God!"

"I just thought I was wealthy, but *now* I have more than enough to meet my family's needs and make our dreams come true — because I am an ample sower toward the work of the Gospel!"

You can live in your financial "afterward" and come out of your situation with great abundance. But you must be teachable and open to receive it. You must hear, receive, and understand the Word of God that comes to you concerning money. And you must act on it in faith and total obedience.

God foretold to Abraham that Abraham's seed would go into captivity, but that they would *afterward* be delivered and come out of bondage with great abundance. Then in Exodus 3:21, after the Israelites' 400-year-long captivity, God describes the event that is about to take place.

A Divine Transaction: The *'How'* of God's Deliverance of His People

Exodus 3:21 says, *"And I will give this people favour in the sight of the Egyptians: and it shall come to pass, that, when ye go, YE SHALL NOT GO EMPTY."* And we know that when God says, "You shall not go out empty," He means every word. Those people could count on going out full!

Now let's look at verse 22, in which God tells Moses how He's going to do it: *"But every woman shall borrow of her neighbour, and of her that sojourneth in her house, jewels of silver, and jewels of gold, and raiment: and ye shall put them upon your sons, and upon your daughters; and ye shall spoil the Egyptians."*

God intended that this transaction "spoil" the Egyptians and make the Israelites rich. It was a *divine transaction* designed to give the children of Israel the "great abundance" God spoke to Abraham about in Genesis 15!

It's Time For *You* To Enter In

Do you think it is a hard thing for God to change your financial status? He can shift your status and change your situation overnight. God is not the problem. The enemy is the god of this world (*see* Second Corinthians 4:4), and the Bible says that he is the thief, the one who steals, kills, and destroys. But it also says that Jesus has come to give us life and to cause us to have it — live it, enjoy it — more abundantly (John 10:10)!

Your problem is never with God. He could blink and change your situation just that fast. It's *you* that needs to submit to, agree with, and cooperate with His laws and ways of doing things. Then change will come. Then you'll hear, "Enter into the joy of the Lord! Enter into the enjoyment of Heavenly resources at your disposal!" (*See* Matthew 25:21 and 23.)

I don't believe when the master said to the faithful stewards, "Enter into the joy of your lord," he meant that they were to enter into just some joyful state of mind. No, when God says to us on this side — while we are on the earth, "Enter into My joy," He's not welcoming us into Heaven's gates; He's welcoming us into the realm of increase, where our joy is made full!

Think about it. It's not a joy to be broke. But it *is* a joy to possess an ample supply and to be able to give into the work of God. It's joy to buy an automobile and pay cash for it. It's joy to pay off your mortgage, to enjoy the increase that God gives so that you can give to others.

Didn't Jesus say in John 16:24, *"...ask, and ye shall receive, THAT YOUR JOY MAY BE FULL"*? Well, isn't it a joy to have your needs met, to receive answers to prayer, to walk in the laws of increase, and to enjoy multiplied abundance?

Many have acted so "spiritual" about the Bible that they've interpreted God's words to fit their religious thinking. But that's not being honest, is it? That's not approaching the Word in simple faith, as a little child, so that the Holy Spirit can teach them.

As for me, I'm going to take God at His Word. God has honored His Word on my behalf for many years. Because I saw prosperity in the Bible and dared to believe that He could change my situation, I am enjoying a state of wealth today that most people only dream about. I've entered in to my "afterward," and my joy is full!

The Role of Expectation In Receiving Your 'Afterward'

God knows ahead of time what He's going to do for you. He knows how He's going to deliver you. Your job is to cooperate with Him, and with your faith and your obedience make the necessary connection that will cause deliverance to come to pass in your life.

I made that statement in a meeting once, and the Holy Spirit quickened a certain passage of Scripture to me.

> *John 6:1-6*
> *1 After these things Jesus went over the sea of Galilee, which is the sea of Tiberias.*
> *2 And a great multitude followed him, because they saw his miracles which he did on them that were diseased.*
> *3 And Jesus went up into a mountain, and there he sat with his disciples.*
> *4 And the passover, a feast of the Jews, was nigh.*
> *5 When Jesus then lifted up his eyes, and saw a great company come unto him, he saith unto Philip, Whence shall we buy bread, that these may eat?*
> *6 AND THIS HE SAID TO PROVE HIM: FOR HE HIMSELF KNEW WHAT HE WOULD DO.*

As you probably know, this passage in John chapter 6 is the account of the feeding of the multitude, in which Jesus fed at least 5,000 people with just two loaves and five fish that God supernaturally multiplied. Jesus asked Philip, "Where are we going to buy bread so that the people may eat?" But Jesus asked the question to prove Philip, because Jesus already knew what He was going to do in order to feed the multitude.

If you're not already living your dreams, God already knows how He's going to get you out of the financial situation you're in. He already knows how He's going to pay off your house! He already knows how He's going to fill your hands with plenty! Will you let Him prove you? Will you past His tests of faith and obedience so that He can do it for you? Will you believe in His willingness and His ability to do it?

What Will God Do For You?

Do you believe you can have great substance? If you don't believe it's possible, then you certainly aren't going to receive from God tomorrow! I have another question for you. Can you *handle* great substance?

To experience handfuls of plenty, you have to be in a position where you're willing and obedient (Isaiah 1:19) — willing to do what God says to do and to go where He says to go, and to do it *willingly*, not begrudgingly.

Then once you have that aspect settled in your heart, you have to think right about money. You can't think religiously about it. You can't think that it's evil or that riches can only belong to just a chosen few. That's why God has given us His Word — so that we can become transformed in our minds from the world's way of thinking to *God's* way of thinking (Romans 12:2). God does not think like we think, so guess who has to change if we want to please Him? *We do!*

Once you've dedicated your heart and your life to obey God willingly, as I said, you're going to have to think correctly about money. You're going to have to *think* right, *believe* right, and *act* right! So there will have to be a certain expectation in your heart about what God will do for you personally.

Looking at the way God prospered people in the Bible will help your faith and expectation, because you know that God doesn't have any favorites. He blessed those who walked with Him in faith and obedience in the Old Testament, and He will bless those who walk with Him in faith and obedience in the *New Testament* (that includes you and me today).

The Greatness of Job

Let's look briefly at a man by the name of Job, who had great possessions. How do we know what Job possessed? Because the Bible tells us. God thought Job's possessions were important enough to place in the pages of the Bible for all to read throughout the ages.

Job 1:1-3
1 There was a man in the land of Uz, whose name was Job; and that man was perfect and upright, and one that feared God, and eschewed evil.
2 And there were born unto him seven sons and three daughters.
3 His substance also was seven thousand sheep, and three thousand camels, and five hundred yoke of oxen, and five hundred she asses, and a very great household; so that this man was the greatest of all the men of the east.

Why did God put this in the Bible? One reason was to show that God favors prosperity. God does not want people to be broke!

Think about the magnitude of Job's possessions! For example, how much food do you think it took just to feed his livestock — 7,000 sheep, 3,000 camels, 500 yoke of oxen, and 500 donkeys?

When you have great possessions as Job did, you have to have some means, or resources, to maintain those possessions.

Counterfeit Prosperity

I know of people today who can't maintain their possessions. I know of those who are living in nice homes they can't afford just to try to show others that they're wealthy. They can't buy window treatments or furniture because they're in over their heads trying to make the house payment each month. They live in a huge house with just a few pieces of furniture inside and sheets on the windows! And it's hot in there in the summer and cold in the winter because they can't pay the utility bills.

On top of that, these people are eating hot dogs, because after they barely make that huge house payment each month, they don't have much of anything left to buy groceries with. They wear glamorous-looking clothes, but don't have anything in their wallets.

There is a "false prosperity" in the land today. People are living large on credit and calling that prosperity. But that wasn't how Job lived. The Word of God states that he had the goods.

The Greatness of Isaac

We read about the greatness of Job. We read in Job 1:3 about Job's possessions: *"His substance also was seven thousand sheep, and three thousand camels, and five hundred yoke of oxen, and five hundred she asses, and a very great household; SO THAT THIS MAN WAS THE GREATEST OF ALL THE MEN OF THE EAST."*

There are other great men of God in the Old Testament we could read about, but let's look for a moment at Isaac, son of Abraham and Sarah. This man grew and increased financially until a king felt threatened by Isaac's wealth.

We can read in Genesis 26 that the king of the Philistines

asked Isaac to leave town because Isaac had become so great in terms of wealth! In essence, King Abimelech said, "Isaac, you've become too great for us. We're feeling threatened. Please leave."

Genesis 26:12-16
12 Then Isaac sowed in that land, and received in the same year an hundredfold: and the Lord blessed him.
13 And the man waxed great, and went forward, and grew until he became very great:
14 For he had possession of flocks, and possession of herds, and great store of servants: and the Philistines envied him.
15 For all the wells which his father's servants had digged in the days of Abraham his father, the Philistines had stopped them, and filled them with earth.
16 And Abimelech said unto Isaac, Go from us; for thou art much mightier than we.

Then later, after Isaac left and settled in a valley, he had another conversation with the king of the Philistines and the king's friend and army captain, and it went something like this: "Now we *really* see that the Lord is with you. Make a treaty with us that you will not harm us."

Genesis 26:26-29
26 Then Abimelech went to him from Gerar, and Ahuzzath one of his friends, and Phichol the chief captain of his army.
27 And Isaac said unto them, Wherefore come ye to me, seeing ye hate me, and have sent me away from you?
28 And they said, We saw certainly that the Lord was with thee: and we said, Let there be now an oath betwixt us,

even betwixt us and thee, and let us make a covenant with thee;

29 That thou wilt do us no hurt, as we have not touched thee, and as we have done unto thee nothing but good, and have sent thee away in peace: thou art now the blessed of the Lord.

Isaac was so blessed that it seemed that every step he made was a "loud" step. Wealth was all around him to the point he and his household and clan became a threat to an entire nation.

What Do You Believe About Your Covenant?

The Bible promises the people of God that they can become lenders, not borrowers — the head and not the tail and above only and not beneath (Deuteronomy 28:13). So why aren't we seeing more of that today among believers? Because the Body of Christ at large doesn't know anything about a new and better covenant established upon better promises (*see* Hebrews 8:6). And among those that do, many "tried" the message, but when things didn't turn around for them when they thought they should, they "quit" the message. Today they are living like any unbeliever — like someone without a covenant — just trying to do the best they can.

Old Covenant men and women who walked with God were blessed materially because they understood the covenant. We need to be dedicated and devoted enough to walk with God, too, and then we need to apply ourselves to the blood of Jesus and to the New Covenant that He ratified and set in motion on our behalf.

The World Will Try To Discourage You and Dampen Your Expectations

Certainly, there are those in this world who are rich, yet who don't walk with God. But the Bible says not to consider them or envy any of their wealth or their ways (Psalm 37:1; Proverbs 24:19).

Let me tell you something else about the world's wealth versus the believers' wealth. When people in the world are blessed, they often flaunt it. In other words, they don't make any apology about having ten cars or five houses, or purses that cost thousands of dollars apiece. But when a Christian makes it big by applying God's laws of prosperity, the enemy doesn't want people to know about that.

If a Christian's wealth does get "played up" in the public eye, the enemy will stir up something to discredit him, accusing him of some kind of wrongdoing just because he's rich. He becomes a target, not because he did anything wrong, but because he's wealthy.

The world has had the notion for so long that Christianity and wealth don't belong together. But they didn't get that idea from the Bible! They got it from doctrines of devils and men, from religious tradition and error. I used to let that bother me, but I don't anymore. And you shouldn't let it bother you, either. When you become wealthy God's way, the world won't always acknowledge that God has blessed you. But there will always be those "warriors" beside you who will shout with you and rejoice over what the Lord has done for you.

Hold Fast to Your Position

When the anointing for wealth — financial favor — is upon you because you understand the covenant, people will give you money. God's glory is upon you because you're believing His holy Word. You will have a story to tell about the Christ life within you. You'll have a spring in your step and a testimony on your lips to the glory of God. And not another day in life will you settle for crumbs under the table, because you know that you have been seated at the Master's table. You know Him intimately as the Shepherd, and in His Presence, you shall have no want (Psalm 23:1). You are living in that realm of "life more abundant," and the wicked one has lost his hold on you!

When you mean business with God, He will prepare you a table in the presence of your enemies (*see* Psalm 23:5). He doesn't mind it when you say to Him, "Lord, I know I'm supposed to be at the table! I'm not moving from my conviction! Get me out of this mess!"

Then hold your ground and refuse to give up your position. God likes it when you stand firm and steady on His Word. Go ahead and make a bold confession, "My enemies thought they had me. They wanted me to stay broke all my life. But God is preparing me a table! I'm breaking loose, and poverty can't hold me!"

I'm talking about *expectation.* In every deliverance the Lord has wrought, He creates an expectation first of what He will do. He did it for the children of Israel before He delivered them with silver and gold from the bondage of Egypt. And He will create a beautiful expectation of the "afterward" He wants to accomplish in *your* life.

How To Know the Best Time To Sow

You may have read this book thinking, *A lot of what this man wrote describes me and my situation. I see the truth concerning sowing and reaping. But I'm hurting financially. This isn't the right time to sow.*

When *is* the best time to sow? *N-o-w.* Right now — not when conditions are favorable — is when you need to sow.

Ecclesiastes 11:4-6
4   He that observeth the wind shall not SOW; and he that regardeth the clouds shall not REAP.

5 As thou knowest not what is the way of the spirit,
nor how the bones do grow in the womb of her that is
with child: even so thou knowest not the works of God
who maketh all.
6 In the morning SOW THY SEED, and in the evening
WITHHOLD NOT THINE HAND: for thou knowest not
whether shall prosper, either this or that, or whether
they both shall be alike good.

The first part of verse 4 says, *"He that observeth the wind shall not sow...."* In other words, he (or she) that gives heed to or regards turbulent, adverse, financial times will not sow. The person who isn't walking by faith, but who's walking according to his circumstances, won't step out and sow.

Sowing is an anointed act of faith that is independent of circumstances. The person whose hands and heart have been anointed to sow depends only on the word of the Lord or the leading of the Spirit to do his sowing.

The Best Time to Sow

Never wait for a good time to sow. If you wait, looking for an "appropriate" time, that time is never going to come! In fact, if a person is in financial straits, waiting to act on this revelation usually only serves to postpone his blessing while his situation gets worse and worse. The "wind" will dictate to him not to sow. If he does manage to sow in faith, he'll need to be careful, or the "clouds" will tell him he can't reap.

Because we live in this world that is governed by the world system, the winds of the adversaries of God's Word will always be blowing — winds of economic experts making frightening predictions, winds of the banking and credit systems hungry for huge profits, and even winds of religious doctrines telling you God doesn't want you to have too much.

The wind is blowing hard and the clouds are hanging heavy when it comes to money and the financial realm. But the Word of God overcomes any wind of adversity, anger, and opposition to its message concerning God's will to prosper you. That Word of Life overpowers clouds of debt, distress, destruction, poverty, and lack. It can bring you into a place where you experience total financial freedom.

If you have God's Word in your heart, you need to look these winds of opposition in the face and defy their arguments against your sowing seed. Then find places to sow — ask God to show you — and don't ever stop sowing.

Then don't permit for one minute the clouds to tell you not to expect your harvest. Those dark clouds of doubt, like a smokescreen, could move in an instant and your harvest appear on the horizon of your life.

Why People Don't Sow

There are many reasons people don't sow into God's Kingdom, and we already looked at a few of them. Some people don't know the truth. Some people know but refuse to grow. They are content to stay where they are in life. And some people are simply stingy.

Now let's look at verse 5 of Ecclesiastes 11.

Ecclesiastes 11:5
As thou knowest not what is the way of the spirit, nor how the bones do grow in the womb of her that is with child: even so thou knowest not the works of God who maketh all.

Many start out sowing because they heard the message concerning sowing and reaping. But then they became discouraged after awhile because their situation didn't turn around when they thought it should. They couldn't see God at work, so they gave up and quit.

But God is always working on your behalf when you walk by faith. You may not always see or even sense right away what He's up to. But like a curtain that opens at show time, there will come a day — if you won't quit — that God will open up that "curtain" and unveil His financial blessing in your life, bringing you to a new level of wealth and of giving.

Ecclesiastes 11:6
In the morning sow thy seed, and in the evening withhold not thine hand: for thou knowest not whether shall prosper, either this or that, or whether they both shall be alike good.

This verse is talking about sowing at all times — "morning and evening." I especially like the phrase, "...*and in the evening WITHHOLD NOT THINE HAND....*" Solomon was talking about sowing — a hand anointed for sowing!

Look at that word "withholding." It's withholding that keeps people broke.

Proverbs 11:24
There is that scattereth [sows, gives, or disperses], and yet increaseth; and there is that withholdeth more than is meet, but it tendeth to poverty.

Then look at the last part of Ecclesiastes 11:6: "...*for thou knowest not whether shall prosper, either this or that, or whether they both shall be alike good.*" This verse says that we don't know which seed is going to be the seed that prospers us, the seed that God uses to bring us from *supply* to *surplus* or from captivity to freedom. That's why the first part of the verse says to sow both in the morning and in the evening.

We could add to that, "Sow in the *north* and sow in the *south*," or, "Sow in the *east* and sow in the *west*," or, "Sow into *this* ministry and sow into *that* ministry." Sometimes God will tell you to sow into people that you don't particularly like. Yet you'll feel the tug of the Holy Ghost on your heart to give. You need to give when you sense that tugging or leading, because that seed might be the one that prospers you as you have never prospered before!

When *Not* To Sow!

We know that *now* is the best time to sow financial seed. But let me share with you when it's *not* the best time to sow! Sometimes we can learn best what to do by learning what *not* to do!

Number One: Sowing Just Because Someone Else Is Sowing

Some people try to sow just because other people are sowing. These people don't have anointed hands or anointed hearts. They don't have a revelation of God's Word in their heart concerning sowing. They don't have an ounce of faith, but they decide they'll "try" sowing to see what it will do for them, because they saw someone else doing it and getting blessed. They try it for a few days or weeks, but then they quit because they're not seeing any results. They're not in faith.

You can't act on another person's revelation and expect faith or the Word of God to work for you. You must act on your own faith in order for faith to profit you.

Number Two: Giving To Receive Attention

Some people will sow money into a minister or a ministry for the purpose of receiving special recognition or preferential treatment. Maybe they want to be friends with the man of God, or maybe they want the best seat in the house at special meetings. But that is not money's purpose. In fact, the Bible says that people who do good things to be seen of men "have their reward already" (*see* Matthew 6:2,5-6). In other words, they don't need to be looking for a harvest or reward from God since accolades and "applause" from men seems to be what they're really seeking after.

Sometimes some of the biggest sowers into my ministry will attend my meetings, and I might not even look at them during a service. They don't mind. They're not sowing financial seed to get my attention; they're sowing because they know the truth, and they're acting on it. They have a revelation and an expectation in their heart of what God will do.

No minister can multiply your seed sown and bring forth a harvest in your life that can completely turn your situation around. But God can! And He will do it, but your attention and expectation must be toward him, not the ministry or the man or woman of God you gave to.

A minister should show gratitude when he or she receives a financial gift, but there comes a time when he has to step back and not interfere with what God is doing in the lives of those who are giving. Although I deeply appreciate the people who give to me, I don't always write thank-you notes to everyone who gives. I always say, "I receive." I don't get caught up in making a fuss over the gift or the giver. If I do, I'll get over into an area of trying to do God's part in their lives. And I guarantee you, these people are not looking for another thank-you note — they're looking to *pay off* some notes! They're looking for a harvest.

I know that if I get caught up over-recognizing people who give to me, it's going to take their attention off the Lord. A minister could over-thank a person who gives to him to the point it drops into that person's spirit one day that it's no longer between him and God; now it's between that person who gave and the minister he gave to.

But the reason that person gave to begin with was, God was doing something in his or her heart. If that person will stay steady in his giving and keep his attention focused on the Word, God will complete the work He began in the heart of that person. *God will bring forth the increase and the harvest, not any man.* The harvest may come from the hands of a man or from a group of people, but the sower who reaps his harvest knows that his blessing came by the hand of God.

Number Three: Giving Because of the Thrill You Feel

I've talked throughout this book about a financial anointing, about anointed giving, and how the anointing can be connected to wealth when your wealth is connected to the Word.

There is an anointing associated with giving and receiving, but your giving and your receiving must be done by *faith.* In other words, the anointing could be present, but if you don't cooperate with that anointing by faith, nothing will happen for you.

This is why people who get in prayer lines to receive the healing anointing — the healing power of God — often don't receive their healing. They don't mix faith with the power. They think that just because they felt the anointing or they "fell under the power," God will just automatically do something for them without their believing anything.

They haven't been taught that after you experience the power of God, you must keep the working of the Holy Spirit alive in your life by faith — by your constant confession of faith in God's Word and in what He is doing in your life. Remember I said that your receiving from God is between you and Him, not between you and any man.

Many people follow "goose bump" preaching, and they'll go from meeting to meeting looking for some kind of a feeling. But goose bumps will keep you broke! If these people want to get past *feeling* and get on to actually *receiving*, they need to get grounded in the Word of God and add some faith to the thrill they feel when the Spirit of God is moving.

Number Four: Giving Only to the Poor and Disregarding the Rich When God Speaks

Many Christians have a problem with sowing into a person who has more than they have. For example, you might see a man wearing a better suit than you're wearing, and the Lord says to you, *"Give him three-hundred dollars."* Would you give the man the money? If so, would you do it willingly?

If you Lord speaks to you to give to someone who's wearing a nice suit, first, you don't know what that man is going through. Second, you don't know what he has been sowing into the lives of others. That's why it's so important just to obey God when He speaks or prompts you to give.

People by nature prefer to give to someone they think is not doing as well as they're doing. Perhaps it has something to do with their ego; they feel better about helping someone out whom they think really needs help.

I'm not saying we're always supposed to sow into those who are doing better than we are. I *am* saying that we need to be led by the Spirit of God in our giving, because at times, God will lead us in that way.

God might lead you to sow "upward," because in sowing upward, you're *sowing* where you want to be *going*! You see others who have been prospered by God, and you're inspired by their testimonies. Then the Holy Spirit sets you up to go there, too, by sowing into their lives in the same way they've sown into the lives of others who inspired them to come up higher.

What About the Poor?

Some in the Body of Christ only want to give to the poor. The Bible has a lot to say about giving to the poor. Certainly, we're not to turn our back on those who can't even feed themselves. However, there are organizations that make a racket out of feeding the poor, but they don't preach the Gospel to the poor after they feed them. They feed them and then those poor people continue to worship cows, cattle, and thousands of other idols and false gods. These groups are feeding them, but they're not doing it in the Name of Jesus, showing them the love of God and the way to eternal salvation.

I know of Christians who for years and years have been sending money to feed poor children because they saw a photo or something on TV that showed a dirty, skinny baby with flies all around him. So these believers got emotional and started sending money. They've been faithful in their giving to these groups, but they haven't prospered significantly in the 30 years they've been giving.

We already looked at giving because of feelings. You can't always go by feelings when you give. Don't misunderstand me. Someone has to feed those starving children. But if all of your money is going toward those types of organizations, you're not sowing for a breakthrough. You might be sowing because you're sensitive or sympathetic. But you might not be anointed to sow where you've been sowing all those years.

There are honest, legitimate organizations out there that feed the poor without trying to "sucker" you — and then they give the poor the Gospel on top of that. If people are starving, you have to feed them so they can listen to you! They can't hear you if they're hungry!

So to feed the poor can be good and right, but we need to attach some wisdom to our giving and be led by the Holy Spirit every time we give.

Number Five: Sowing Into 'Questionable Ground'

Sowing into questionable ground goes right along with leaning to your own understanding concerning giving, and giving based on feelings and misinformation, as we just saw in the last two sections.

As we saw in Ecclesiastes 11:6, you don't know whether "this seed or that" is going to prosper for you. In other words, some seed you've sown isn't going to do anything for you. Does that mean you should stop sowing? No! You need to keep on sowing, developing yourself in following the leading of the Holy Spirit, who will never steer you wrong in your giving.

I know I have sowed some "bad" seed in the past; I've sown into people I shouldn't have given to. Some seed I wish I could go and get back! In my eagerness to sow and to obey God, I opened my hands quickly to sow in those instances, and the Holy Spirit simply wasn't leading me.

But I've sown countless good seeds too! I really don't regret any of the "bad" seed, because I consider those mistakes as part of the learning process.

When you partner with God in your giving, God can and will do the impossible for you. He will partner with you as He did with Abraham and other men and women of old who made the commitment to trust God and obey Him in everything.

No matter what your situation today, you can do better,

and God is calling you up higher. He wants you to declare by faith, "No more empty hands!" and then to live out the reality of that truth every day of your life.

Prayer of Salvation

A born-again, committed relationship with God is the key to the victorious life. Jesus, the Son of God, laid down His life and rose again so that we could spend eternity with Him in Heaven and experience His absolute best on earth. The Bible says, *"For God so loved the world, that he gave his only begotten Son, that whosoever believeth in him should not perish, but have everlasting life"* (John 3:16).

It is the will of God that everyone receive eternal salvation. The way to receive this salvation is to call upon the name of Jesus and confess Him as your Lord. The Bible says, *"That if thou shalt confess with thy mouth the Lord Jesus, and shalt believe in thine heart that God hath raised him from the dead, thou shalt be saved. For whosoever shall call upon the name of the Lord shall be saved"* (Romans 10:9-10,13).

Jesus has given salvation, healing, and countless benefits to all who call upon His Name. These benefits can be yours if you receive Him into your heart by praying this prayer:

Father God,

> *I come to You right now as a sinner. Right now, I choose to turn away from sin, and I ask You to cleanse me of all unrighteousness. I believe that Your Son, Jesus, died on the Cross to take away my sins. I also believe that He rose again from the dead so that I might be justified and made righteous through faith in Him. I call upon the Name of Jesus Christ for salvation. I want Him to be the Savior and Lord of my life. Jesus, I choose to follow You, and ask that You fill me with the power of the Holy Spirit. I declare that right now, I am a born-*

again child of God. I am free from sin and full of the
righteousness of God. I am saved in Jesus' Name. Amen.

If you have prayed this prayer to receive Jesus Christ into your life, we would like to hear from you. Please write us at:

Ever Increasing Word Ministries
P.O. Box 7
Darrow, LA 70725

About the Author

D r. Leroy Thompson, Sr. is the pastor and founder of Word of Life Christian Center in Darrow, Louisiana, a growing and thriving body of believers from various walks of life. He has been in the ministry since 1973, serving as a pastor since 1976. Even though he completed his undergraduate degree and theology doctorate and was an instructor for several years at a Christian Bible college in Louisiana, it wasn't until 1983, when he received the baptism in the Holy Spirit, that the revelation knowledge of God's Word changed his life; and it continues to increase his ministry. Dr. Thompson attributes the success of his life and ministry to his reliance on the Word of God, being filled with the Holy Spirit, and being led by the Spirit of God. Today Dr. Thompson travels across the United States taking the message of ministerial excellence, dedication, and discipline to the Body of Christ.

To contact Dr. Leroy Thompson, Sr.,

write:

Dr. Leroy Thompson, Sr.

Ever Increasing Word Ministries

P. O. Box 7

Darrow, Louisiana 70725

Please include your prayer requests

and comments when you write.

Other Books by Dr. Leroy Thompson, Sr.

Money Cometh to the Body of Christ!

Money With a Mission

What To Do When Your Faith Is Challenged

*The Voice of Jesus — Speaking
God's Word With Authority*

Becoming a Commander of Covenant Wealth

Money, Thou Art Loosed!

How To Find Your Wealthy Place

I'll Never Be Broke Another Day In My Life

Order these books and other products by
Dr. Leroy Thompson online at www.eiwm.org.

The Ever Increasing Word Ministries Vision

Changing

the Lives of People

With the Word of God

AND

Equipping

the Body of Christ

To Evangelize the World